Games, Crowdbreakers and Community Builders

Jim Burns

GENERAL EDITOR

COMPILED BY

Mark Simone and Joel Lusz

Gospel Light

Gospel Light is an evangelical Christian publisher dedicated to serving the local church. We believe God's vision for Gospel Light is to provide church leaders with biblical, user-friendly materials that will help them evangelize, disciple and minister to children, youth and families.

We hope this Gospel Light resource will help you discover biblical truth for your own life and help you minister to youth. God bless you in your work.

For a free catalog of resources from Gospel Light please contact your Christian supplier or call 1-800-4-GOSPEL.

PUBLISHING STAFF
William T. Greig, Publisher
Dr. Elmer L. Towns, Senior Consulting Publisher
Dr. Gary S. Greig, Senior Consulting Editor
Jill Honodel, Editor
Pam Weston, Assistant Editor
Kyle Duncan, Associate Publisher
Bayard Taylor, M.Div., Editor, Theological and Biblical Issues
Debi Thayer, Designer

ISBN 0-8307-1881-8
© 1997 by Jim Burns
All rights reserved.
Printed in U.S.A.

HOW TO MAKE CLEAN COPIES FROM THIS BOOK

Contents

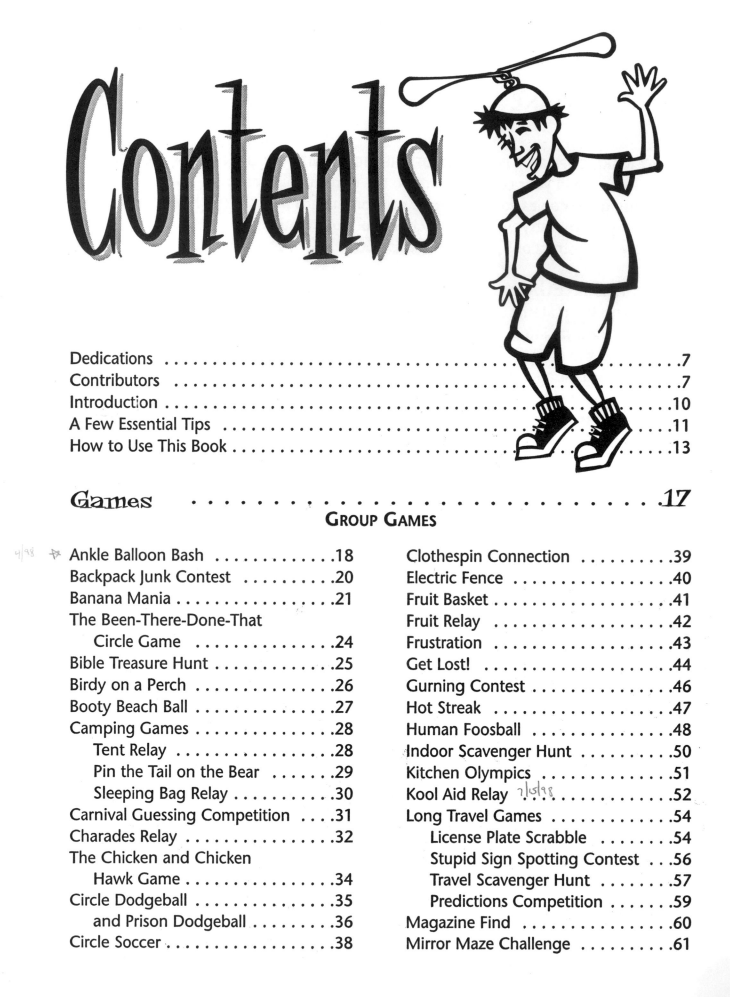

IMPROMPTU GAMES

Crowdbreakers 125

Community Builders · · · · · · · · · · · · · · · · 165

Indexes ·208

Dedications

This book is dedicated to some amazing women who have given of themselves to me in the nurturing, selfless manner that has somehow become "out of vogue" among women these days. In a time when our youth are starving for love and nurture, I can thank God that my life has been filled with so many loving, supportive women of God. Through them and their strength I have found much of who I am in Christ.

My grandmothers: Valeria Schlauch, Catherine Simone, Elizabeth Morton, Ann Gladish.

My mothers: Marilyn Floyd, Becky Gladish.

My daughters: Lindsey Simone, Erin Simone.

My sisters-in-law: Anne Heithecker, Michelle Simone, Gail Simone.

Sisters in ministry: Terri Thomas, Kim Lockert, Ruth Seton, Priscilla Norling, Helen Pointer.

My dear little friend: Heidi Burns.

My friends and coworkers in Christ: Betty Mitchell, Margery Cowan, Jane Thomas, Pat Nichols, Mary Bourisseau, Marge Weygandt, Sandy Caniglia, Betsy Whitmore, Mary Maske, Pixie Ferlito and Shirley Tyler.

And most especially, my wife, Kathy, who is akin to the woman of Proverbs 31. Some are still living and loving me; some have gone on to love me through their memory and now stand with God. All have immeasurably blessed me and helped me to define my life that I may touch others. When my hands comfort others in ministry, it is because their hands taught me how.

—Mark A. Simone

To Angie,
Thanks for giving me Koral. I love you.

—Joel

Contributors

Mark Simone has been ministering to students in Ohio for nearly 18 years. He is the author of *Ministering to Kids Who Don't Fit* (Accent Publications, 1993) and *Teaching Today's Youth* (Accent, 1996, coauthored with wife, Kathy). He wishes that one day all of the students he has worked with will send him to Italy for a vacation.

Joel Lusz has been in youth ministry for 16 years and is serving as Family Life Pastor at Palm Beach Community since hearing his call to sun, surf and sand. Joel suffers for Jesus in Florida with his wife Angie and daughter Koral.

Eric and Starr Wrisley are currently raising support to go to Holland with Christian Associates International to plant high-impact churches. Some have accused them of praying too hard for a baby, as they are now expecting twins.

Russ Van Nest is a veteran youth pastor of eight years working in western Pennsylvania, and is also the president of Everything Under The Son Ministries, working to equip churches in youth ministry excellence. He is known among his youth group students for offering what is often referred to as Stupid Russ Games.

John Moores is a youth pastor and juvenile probation officer in western Pennsylvania. He is an honorary member of the Deep Creek Lake Polar Bear Club.

Diana Weber-Gardner is marketing manager for Penton Publishing and an artist/communicator who studied for a time at Oxford University in England. Mother and wife, she has also used her being an anomaly of science—being an identical twin—to trick her twin sister's family into thinking she *was* her sister.

Scott Rubin is Director of Student Ministries at The Village Church in Rancho Santa Fe, California. He has been known to refer to his wife and his golden retriever in the same breath.

Daiv Whaley is a writer and youth worker who works with emotionally troubled children. He resides in the beautiful hills of Akron, Ohio, where he writes short stories and articles about modern rock music.

Jonathan Traux is a youth pastor who, after four years of ministry, is just beginning to learn the lessons his teenagers are trying to teach him. He lives in Louisville, Ohio, with his wife, Debbie, and his son, Daniel.

Tom Patterson is a pastor in California who has ministered to teenagers in the continental United States, Alaska, Eastern Europe and the Ukraine. An avid rock climber, Tom can say "I do not like raisins" in 12 different languages.

Troy Scott, an 11-year youth ministry veteran, works with teenagers in the Washington, D.C. metro area. A husband and father of two, one of his favorite ways to spend his time is hanging out with his family, especially if it includes WWF wrestling, which he watches in his underwear with his son, Caleb.

Kipp Smith, a 15-year youth ministry veteran, has spent the last 11 years in youth ministry as Student Pastor at Westside Church in Omaha, Nebraska. Kipp enjoys spending his free time with his wife, Regina, and three children, Azia, Britta and Micah.

Matt Harrison is a consultant to the health care industry, serving the United States and international markets as a long-time youth advisor. In his spare time he plays middle fielder (now called center field) on an 1860s vintage baseball team.

Matt Hoyt and his wife, Melinda, live in Southern California. Matt has been involved in youth ministry for more than seven years. Most recently he has served at Burbank Presbyterian.

Introduction

Let's face it, most of us are on the lookout for fresh ways to get our youth groups interacting and having fun. This resource not only gives you some of the finest ideas in games, crowdbreakers and community builders known in the youth world, it is laid out in the easiest format that I've ever seen!

This resource is divided into easy-to-use categories with plenty of icons that tell you instantly how much time you need to prepare, how much cleanup is involved and even what the gross factor is! We also have an index at the back that gives a brief description of each game so that you don't have to read the whole game to get a quick picture. And to make things easy on you when you're in a hurry, we've devised an index that tells you immediately how much preparation time each activity takes so that when you don't have much time, you know exactly which games, crowdbreakers or community builders to go to and which page they are on.

But this book is not just about fun and games. When a youth group experiences enjoyable times together, the students will be ready to study the Word and participate in the church to a greater extent. So, here's to a good time, even at church!

—Jim Burns

A Few Essential Tips

ADAPT

Read the material, then ask yourself "How can I use this with my group? What should I add? What should I take away? How can it be adapted for our group?" In other words, change it to fit your students. Change the language. Update the material. Use the right props and costumes. Adjust. Alter. Tailor-make. Custom-fit. Modify. Adapt!

USE PROPS AND COSTUMES

Budget some money for buying costuming paraphernalia—dresses, hats, boots, jackets, purses, wigs, oversized clothes, telephones, musical instruments, drums, eyeglasses, sports equipment, etc. Ask church members to donate discards or leftovers from garage sales. Ninety percent of the success of a skit rests with the costuming and props.

Last year I took $200 out of the youth ministry budget and went thrift-shopping. My first stop was the thrift store. After that, I hit garage sales, 99¢ stores, any place with cheap stuff. You'd be amazed at how many good skit props you can buy at places like that with little money. If you're going to do a cowboy skit, get cowboy hats, boots, holsters, vests and whatever else. Make it more real, yet outrageous. Something about putting on costumes helps students loosen up and get into the spirit of the fun.

Swallow Your Own Pride

If you can't be a fool for Christ, then whose fool are you? Go ahead and put on the makeup, get hit in the face with a pie, put mustard under your arms. Who cares?! This is how walls are broken down and relationships are built. Set an example of fun for your students. Go for it!

Keep a Record

Have you ever wondered if you have already done a skit or played a game or given a message to the group you're meeting with today? Us too. We have tried to make record keeping as simple and convenient as possible. Next to each activity, message or skit you use, write the date and with which group it was used. You can also jot down notes for new ideas or suggestions for adaptations or improvements.

—Mark Simone and Joel Lusz

How to Use This Book

There are two game sections: "Group Games," and "Impromptu Games." The Group Games are for the entire group. Impromptu Games call for a few volunteers to do the activity in front of the group. Most of the Impromptu Games have a surprise for at least one of the suckers, I mean participants.

The activities are arranged alphabetically, or you can find the game that's right for your event by using the "Topical Guide" and the Index of "Preparation Times".

Check out the icon descriptions on the next page! The icons give you clues about each game or activity—for example, check out the gross factor, how much preparation time you will need, or even how much cleanup is needed.

Icon Descriptions

NUMBER

SMALL GROUP (LESS THAN 10)

MEDIUM GROUP (10-30 PEOPLE)

LARGE GROUP (MORE THAN 30)

ANY SIZE GROUP

PREP TIME

Includes setup and preparation, such as measuring, drawing, cooking, etc. It does *not* include the time required for gathering or shopping for the materials needed.

TIME REQUIRED

Approximate time the activity takes, including giving directions and forming teams if necessary. Time based on semi-cooperative kids.

PLAYING FIELDS

Indoor activity

Outdoor activity

Indoor or **Outdoor** activity

ACTIVITY LEVELS

Low Activity: Staying in seats with little movement

Medium Activity: Some walking or movement

High Activity: Lots of running, movement and noise

CLEANUP

Little to no cleanup

A little messy, needing a towel or sponge

Messy, a multi-toweler with sponges

Get out the hose and shovels!

GROSS FACTOR

(the degree of yuck)

None to very little

A little nauseating

Disgusting

Not for the faint of heart

SPECIAL REQUIREMENTS

(e.g. a large room, recycled materials or cold weather)

Games

game \gām\ *n* **1 a** : activity engaged in for diversion or amusement: PLAY (from *Merriam Webster's Collegiate Dictionary, Tenth Edition*)

Games aren't just a fun way to fill time. They have a purpose. Games can build a stronger group and help develop friendships. They put the seriousness of life on hold and give students opportunities to let off steam. The games have been divided into two categories. "Group Games" are games that everyone can participate in. "Impromptu Games," on the other hand, are those in which a few students participate while the rest of the group watch. These may appear to the students to be spontaneous, even though you have taken the time to prepare. Either way, your students are going to have a great time!

As a trainer for the National Institute of Youth Ministry, I was speaking at a conference for youth and their adult leaders in Poland several years ago when I discovered that these folks don't play games. So, spilling into an abandoned parking lot, we led these wonderful Polish Christian youth and their leaders in as many new games as we could remember. It will remain one of the most meaningful memories of my nearly two decades of youth work.

Games are not wasted time; they bring people together in time spent sharing fun and enjoying life.

—Mark Simone

SPECIAL FEATURES

NUMBER
15-50 PEOPLE

PREP TIME
1-5 MINUTES

TIME REQUIRED
15-30 MINUTES

IN/OUTDOOR
IN OUT

ACTIVITY LEVEL

CLEANUP LEVEL

GROSS FACTOR

Ankle Balloon Bash

This game works best in a large room or gymnasium.

MATERIALS NEEDED

String or narrow gift-wrapping ribbon
Several pairs of scissors
Lots of balloons, at least one for each person

HOW TO PLAY

Provide each player with about a three-foot length of string and one balloon. Tell them to blow up their balloons as large as possible (without popping). Then everyone removes their shoes and ties one end of the string to the balloon and the other end to their ankles. Have adult leaders help. The object of the game is to have each student try to pop the other students' balloons without having his or her own balloon popped. When a person's balloon is popped, he or she cannot pop any more balloons and must leave the playing area and sit down. The last person standing with a balloon still around his or her ankle wins.

Variations

- Guys vs. girls
- Adults vs. students
- Play this in total darkness or with a strobe light on
- Divide students into teams and give each team a different color of balloons, i.e. Team A has red, Team B has blue. The last team to have a balloon unpopped is the winning team.
- Divide students into two teams. Have the two teams line up across from each other on opposite sides of the room. Then at your signal both teams run across the room to the other side. While they are running across the room, they try to pop as many balloons as possible. Each person whose balloon is popped is out and must sit down. Last unpopped player wins for the team.
- Another variation for team play requires a center dividing line down the middle of the playing area. There also needs to be a designated goal on opposite sides of the room. One team will arrange

itself by having its members spread out on their side of the playing area while the other team is selecting a raider. When both teams are ready, the raiding team sends its raider to run across to the other side of the playing area. The raider tries to stomp on as many of the opposing team's balloons as he or she can while the opposition tries to stomp on the raider's balloon. Anyone whose balloon was popped is out of the game. If the raider makes it to the designated goal on the other side of the playing area without losing his or her balloon, he or she is safe and can either stay there or walk back to his or her team without being accosted. If the raider's balloon is popped, then he or she is out of play and sits down. The first team to lose all of its balloons is the loser.

SPECIAL FEATURES

NUMBER

15-50 PEOPLE

PREP TIME

5-10 MINUTES

TIME REQUIRED

15-30 MINUTES

IN/OUTDOOR

IN OUT

ACTIVITY LEVEL

CLEANUP LEVEL

GROSS FACTOR

Backpack Junk Contest

PREPARATION

The week before this activity, tell the students to bring to the next meeting their backpacks filled with silly, wacky, stupid stuff.

Before the meeting, create a list of just about anything a teenager might have in his or her backpack. Your list may include things such as:

ticket stubs	collector cards
empty lunch sack	one dirty sock
pocket Bible	fast food wrapper
toy	guitar pick
lip balm	empty candy or snack wrapper
detention slip	soda cap
comic book	hairbrush

HOW TO PLAY

The game is simple: Ask for items you suspect the students might have in their backpacks. Give prizes to those who show the object mentioned, or give points to those who show the objects first. Give a prize to the one who has the most points at the end of the game.

Variation

This could be turned into a race if you have access to a gymnasium. Line students up along one wall and have them place their backpacks against the opposite wall. After you give the instruction to find a certain object, they must race to their backpacks to find the item, then back to you to prove they have the item.

You can finish with the group voting for the most unusual, the grossest, the most imaginative, the dirtiest, the smelliest, etc. backpacks.

Banana Mania

This game has been successfully used in conjunction with a new programming year Kick-Off Rally.

Much can be done with decorations to add fun and excitement to the event—hang up plastic or cardboard bananas at the door, run yellow streamers everywhere, play banana music—*Day-O!, Yes, We Have No Bananas*—and making an enormous banana split using a new rain gutter for the "dish."

MATERIALS NEEDED

Lots and lots of bananas
Several varieties of ice cream
Several kinds of ice cream toppings
Banana decorations, music, yellow crepe paper streamers
A length of new rain gutter lined with plastic wrap
Plastic spoons
Several large plastic bowls
Strips of cloth for tying hands together

HOW TO BEGIN

Share the following list with the whole group:

Top Ten Reasons
We Are Having Banana Night

10. Incredible "Buy one banana, get 79 free!" sale at the grocery store.
9. Bananas are a lesser known "Fruit of the Spirit."
8. Bananas don't get stuck in your teeth like corn-on-the-cob.
7. Asparagus Night just doesn't have a ring to it.
6. Bananas can be eaten by spiritual infants.
5. While wars glorify violence, bananas could be the international symbol for peace.
4. The Lion King's Rafiki loves squashed bananas.
3. There are no dietary restrictions against bananas in the Bible.
2. We like the song *Day-O!*
1. We wanted to do something with great "a-peel."

SPECIAL FEATURES

NUMBER
15-50 PEOPLE

PREP TIME
60 MINUTES

TIME REQUIRED
60 MINUTES

IN/OUTDOOR
IN OUT

ACTIVITY LEVEL

CLEANUP LEVEL

GROSS FACTOR

REQUIREMENTS

THE GAMES

PREPARATION

Set up an obstacle course using chairs, cones, etc. If the event is outdoors, you can make the course over rough terrain instead.

To play Banana Mania, divide group into fairly equally numbered teams. Each team should give themselves a banana-related name—The Peels, Big Yellow, etc.

Round 1:
The Bananapolis
500 Relay

Have team members line up behind one another. The first person in each team—while doing his or her best monkey imitation—runs through an obstacle course carrying a banana, returns to his or her team and passes the banana baton to the next member who then runs through the obstacle course. Warn them to not abuse the banana!

Round 2:
Four-Legged
Banana Race

Two members of each team peel a banana, then each one grasps one end of the banana in their mouths. They must run through the obstacle course without dropping or breaking the banana. If they do break it, they must get a new banana and start again from where they dropped the first banana. When the first pair completes the course, they run back (without the banana) and tag the hands of the next pair on their team. Each pair repeats the process. All members of each team must run the Four-Legged Banana Race at least once.

Round 3:
Peeling Contest

With hands tied behind their backs, team members must race to a pile of unpeeled bananas, select a banana using their tied-up hands, peel it completely to the satisfaction of the judge and deliver the banana to the team's bowl. They return to the line where the next member's hands are tied and sent off to peel a banana. These peeled bananas can later be used in the banana splits—as long as they don't touch the ground!

SUGGESTIONS

This is a great event to involve parents as helpers (or even involve them in the teams). You *will need* lots of help!

If you plan on making a huge banana split, ask each student to bring either an ice cream topping or a half-gallon of ice cream to the meeting. Shop around for quantities of bananas. Pray for a great sale on bananas! You'll need lots of them!

* Baby Food Relay (pg. 92)

* Banana Split (pg 95)

* Banana Contest (pg 96)

The Been-There-Done-That Circle Game

MATERIALS NEEDED

Chairs for everyone

HOW TO PLAY

Set up a circle with chairs, having one less chair than the number of participants. In the center of the circle one person stands and tells something about him- or herself (something he or she has done, or some place he or she has been, etc.) For example, someone could say, "I've been to the Grand Canyon." Anyone who has *not* been to the Grand Canyon must get up and run for another chair. The person in the middle then has the opportunity to sit down in the circle at this time. When the chairs are full, the one remaining up becomes It and must tell something about him- or herself.

One rule: They may not move to the chairs on either side of them when they are vacated. They must get up and run for another.

Bible Treasure Hunt

10/98

This game is a combination of Bible study, deduction and a race to beat the other groups to the prize.

MATERIALS NEEDED

> A Bible for each team
> Slips of paper for Scripture references

PREPARATION

Use a concordance to find words and Scripture references for clues to various places around your church or ministry location. To get you started, here are a few suggested locations and matching references:

John 19:25	near the cross
Luke 22:12	the upper room
Isaiah 7:11	sign
Psalm 36:9	fountain
Acts 17:23	altar
Genesis 2:9	tree
Psalm 62:3	fence
Matthew 27:10	field
Matthew 16:18	rock

You will need to give the first clue to all of the teams at the same time. The remaining clues will need to be hidden around the church in the various locations.

HOW TO PLAY

Divide students into teams. Give all of the teams the first clue. Using the Scripture clues you have prepared ahead of time, teams must go to the suggested location to receive the next clue. The first group to reach the final destination wins the event.

Variation

If you only have two teams, give each team a different set of clues, but the same destination.

SPECIAL FEATURES

NUMBER
10-50 PEOPLE

PREP TIME
30-60 MINUTES

TIME REQUIRED
20 MINUTES

INDOOR

ACTIVITY LEVEL

CLEANUP LEVEL

GROSS FACTOR

SPECIAL FEATURES

NUMBER
15-100 PEOPLE

PREP TIME
NONE

TIME REQUIRED
10-15 MINUTES

IN/OUTDOOR
IN OUT

ACTIVITY LEVEL

CLEANUP LEVEL

GROSS FACTOR

Birdy on a Perch

This is another fun game that involves the whole group.

HOW TO PLAY

Have all of the guys form a circle. Then have all of the girls form a circle around the guys with one girl standing behind each guy. The guy in front of a girl is now that girl's partner. If you have an uneven number of guys and girls, you may have to have extras sit out, use leaders and parents to even it out, or divide students by age/size.

Explain that the girls are going to start walking in a clockwise direction and the guys are going to walk in the opposite (counterclockwise) direction. When the leader yells "Birdy on a perch," the guy is to get down on all fours and his partner has to run back to him and sit on his back. The last girl to sit down is out along with her partner. This continues until there is only one pair left!

Variation

You can give the game a new face by naming it something else. For example, you could call this "surfer on a board." Anything that makes it appropriate for your group!

Booty
Beach Ball

SPECIAL FEATURES

NUMBER

15-30 PEOPLE

PREP TIME

10 MINUTES

TIME REQUIRED

30 MINUTES

IN/OUTDOOR

ACTIVITY LEVEL

CLEANUP LEVEL

GROSS FACTOR

MATERIALS NEEDED

Large beach ball
Volleyball net or long rope
Several bedsheets or similar covering

PREPARATION

This can be played outside on a grass or sand volleyball court, or it can be played indoors in a large enough room to accommodate the whole group. Prepare the playing area by stringing the volleyball net (or a rope) across the middle of the playing area, then drape the sheets (or similar covering) over the net (or rope) so that the two sides can not see each other

HOW TO PLAY

Divide the group into two teams, assigning each team to its side of the net. Have the students sit down on their "booties" (bottoms) facing the draped net. Play with the beach ball using regular volleyball rules *except* all the players must remain sitting at all times *and* they can hit the ball as many times as they wish. Score just as a regular volleyball game. Everything else is in play (chairs, lights, wall, people, sound equipment, etc.). Have adult leaders (or non-players) return out-of-bounds balls so that the players can remain seated. Play till one team reaches a score of 15, then have teams switch sides and play again. Or rotate in a new team to challenge the winners.

SPECIAL FEATURES

NUMBER
15-50 PEOPLE

PREP TIME
NONE

TIME REQUIRED
15-20 MINUTES

IN/OUTDOOR
IN OUT

ACTIVITY LEVEL

CLEANUP LEVEL

GROSS FACTOR

REQUIREMENTS

Camping Games

A camping theme can be incorporated into a lock-in (all-nighter), retreat or regular youth group games and activities.

Tent Relay

MATERIALS NEEDED

Two identical two- or three-person tents
Optional: A stopwatch

Divide the group into at least two teams, then divide each team in half. The first half of each team will race to put up the tent and the second half of the team will race to take it down, delivering the disassembled and packed away tent to a designated finish line.

It's really interesting to watch the students trying to work together as a team and still do it quickly. The best part is watching them try to squeeze the tent back into its bag.

Option: If you want to have more than two teams or there is only one tent available, you can time each team—the one with the fastest time wins.

Pin the Tail
on the Bear

The title of this game makes it sound like "Pin the Tail on the Donkey"—and it is! When was the last time your grown-up high school students played pin the tail on anything?

MATERIALS NEEDED

One sheet of poster board
Several sheets of brown construction paper
Scissors
Pins, tacks or transparent tape
A blindfold

PREPARATION
Draw a huge bear on the sheet of poster board—without a tail, of course! Make several copies of a tail on the brown construction paper and cut them out (students can do this for you). Attach the bear poster to a bulletin board (if you use pins or tacks to attach the tails) or wall (use tape for attaching the tails).

HOW TO PLAY
Give each player a tail with a pin, tack or tape. The first player is blindfolded, then turned around a couple of times, pointed toward the poster. He or she walks toward the poster with the tail in his or her outstretched hand. Don't let the player use his or her empty hand to feel along the wall. The player must walk straight ahead and stick the tail where it first touches the wall.

SPECIAL FEATURES

NUMBER
15-50 PEOPLE

PREP TIME
30 MINUTES

TIME REQUIRED
15 MINUTES

INDOOR

ACTIVITY LEVEL

CLEANUP LEVEL

GROSS FACTOR

SPECIAL FEATURES

NUMBER
15+ PEOPLE

PREP TIME
NONE

TIME REQUIRED
15 MINUTES

INDOOR
IN

ACTIVITY LEVEL

CLEANUP LEVEL

GROSS FACTOR

REQUIREMENTS

Sleeping Bag Relay

MATERIALS NEEDED

Sleeping Bags

Take any relay race and alter it by making the students stand in their sleeping bags as they do it. For example: Have them do a gunny sack race where they hop along in their sleeping bags and back to their starting position, then get out of the sleeping bag and the next person jumps in and continues.

Nearly any game can be adapted to a camping theme.

Carnival Guessing Competition

MATERIALS NEEDED

Cheap carnival-type toys

HOW TO PLAY

Select two outgoing group members who will serve as barkers—the person at a circus or carnival who entices you to play a game or see a show. The barker may also guess various facts about a contestant, such as weight or age. The contestant pays a price and the barker guesses. If the barker is correct, the contestant loses. If the barker is wrong, the contestant wins a cheesy prize.

After you have chosen the barkers, ask them to leave the room and then divide the group into two teams. Each team is represented by one of the barkers, but it is important that the barkers have no clue as to who is on their team. Once the teams are selected, ask the barkers to return. The team members line up and the barkers guess the weight (within 5 pounds), the month of birth (within one month either way), or the first letter of the middle name of each member.

If the barker is correct, his or her team gets a point. If the barker is wrong, the student gets to select from a box of junky, cheesy prizes.

The team with the most points wins the competition.

SPECIAL FEATURES

NUMBER
20-50 PEOPLE

PREP TIME
NONE

TIME REQUIRED
20 MINUTES

IN/OUTDOOR
IN OUT

ACTIVITY LEVEL

CLEANUP LEVEL

GROSS FACTOR

SPECIAL FEATURES

NUMBER
10-100 PEOPLE

PREP TIME
15 MINUTES

TIME REQUIRED
30-60 MINUTES

IN/OUTDOOR

ACTIVITY LEVEL

CLEANUP LEVEL

GROSS FACTOR

Charades Relay

PREPARATION

The following sample checklist can be adapted to suit your group. It is scored by the leader who is giving the clues. The first team to successfully get through the list wins. As you can see, the teams need to be separated because they are both working on the same titles. Customize the list to fit your group.

SAMPLE CHECKLIST

Charades Relay Titles

Team A	The Title	Team B
_____	TV: *Gilligan's Island*	_____
_____	Movie: *The Little Mermaid*	_____
_____	Song: "I Want to Hold Your Hand"	_____
_____	Movie: *Wizard of Oz*	_____
_____	TV: *The Brady Bunch*	_____
_____	Song: "Jesus Freak"	_____
_____	Book: *Green Eggs and Ham*	_____
_____	TV: *Mission Impossible*	_____
_____	Movie: *Star Wars*	_____
_____	Song: "Jesus Loves Me"	_____
_____	TV: *Looney Tunes*	_____
_____	Movie: *Jurassic Park*	_____
_____	Song: "Surfin' USA"	_____
_____	Book: *Treasure Island*	_____
_____	TV: *ER*	_____
_____	Movie: *Beauty and the Beast*	_____
_____	Book: *The Cat in the Hat*	_____
_____	TV: *The Flintstones*	_____
_____	Movie: *Gone with the Wind*	_____
_____	Song: "Singin' in the Rain"	_____
_____	Song: "Save the Last Dance for Me"	_____

HOW TO PLAY

Divide students into two or more teams. Have each team select a team captain. The team captains come to the leader for the first title, and they are instructed to enforce the normal rules of charades (no talking, etc.) within their team—or have adult leaders or nonparticipating students monitor the groups. At the signal from the leader, they run back to the area assigned to their group and begin to perform their charade. Each group needs to be an equal distance from its leader and in an area where they cannot see or hear the other teams. The first student to answer correctly runs to the leader for the second title. The process continues until one of the teams completes the list.

SPECIAL
FEATURES

NUMBER

10-100 PEOPLE

PREP TIME

5 MINUTES

TIME REQUIRED

20-30 MINUTES

OUTDOOR

OUT

ACTIVITY LEVEL

CLEANUP LEVEL

GROSS FACTOR

The Chicken and Chicken Hawk Game

OBJECT OF THE GAME:

To be the last chicken who hasn't had his or her egg smashed by a chicken hawk.

MATERIALS NEEDED

A large outside playing area
One raw egg for all but two players
One knee-high nylon stocking for all but two players

DIRECTIONS

Appoint two or more students (depending on the size of your group) to be the Chicken Hawks. Everyone else is a Chicken. All of the Chickens put their eggs in the toes of their stocking and pull the stocking over their heads until the egg is resting in the center of their heads. You know the stocking is on correctly if the students look like bank robbers with an egg on top of their heads.

All of the Chickens line up at one end of the playing area. The Chicken Hawks stand in the center of the playing area.

At a given signal the Chickens run past the Chicken Hawks to the other side of the playing area, trying to avoid having their eggs smashed by the Hawks. The Hawks are allowed to slap the eggs with their hands. A gentle hit does the trick—no need to slam the egg.

Once a Chicken has had his or her egg smashed, he or she becomes a Chicken Hawk. The winner is the last Chicken to have his or her egg smashed.

Circle Dodgeball

This game can be played inside or out. Many of the students may have played this game in elementary school.

MATERIALS NEEDED

A large, soft playground ball (the kind used in elementary schools)

HOW TO PLAY

Have the whole group form a circle. Choose about one-quarter to one-half of the students to stand inside the large circle. Now play dodgeball with the students on the outside of the circle trying to hit the students on the inside. When a student gets hit, he or she is out and joins those forming the circle. They can still participate by trying to hit those who are left in the middle. The last student standing in the middle wins.

Variations

- Use more than one ball
- Use different types and sizes of balls
- Guys vs. girls
- Adults vs. students
- Throw with opposite hand

SPECIAL FEATURES

NUMBER
20-100 PEOPLE

PREP TIME
1-5 MINUTES

TIME REQUIRED
15-30 MINUTES

IN/OUTDOOR
IN OUT

ACTIVITY LEVEL

CLEANUP LEVEL

GROSS FACTOR

9/98

Prison Dodgeball

Prison Dodgeball is a fun variation of Dodgeball. Many students may have played this in elementary school and there may be different regional versions of the rules. The students will let you know!

MATERIALS NEEDED

A large, soft playground ball

PREPARATION

Draw (with a stick in the dirt or with chalk on a hard surface) a large rectangle about the size of a volleyball court with side lines, center line and a back line. If for some reason you can't draw a court, lay rope or string down on the ground to indicate the lines, or you can use a volleyball court (without the net) or a basketball court.

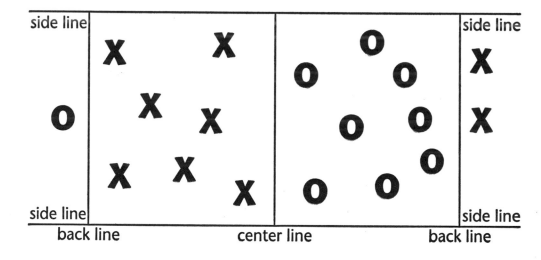

HOW TO PLAY

Form two teams and have them face each other with a dividing line down the center. The two teams face each other and throw the ball back and forth at each other. If a student is hit with the ball, that student is out. That person then goes behind the opposing team's back line and is allowed to catch the ball and continue to hit the opposing team members. Eventually, the game has a few students remaining on

each team's side, and the students who have gotten out standing behind the back line still able to throw at the opposing team. The team with the last player remaining in the court wins.

Variations

- Use more than one ball.
- If a ball is caught before it bounces, the person who threw the ball is out instead of the person who caught it.
- Guys vs. girls
- Adults vs. students

SPECIAL FEATURES

NUMBER
20-30 PEOPLE

PREP TIME
1 MINUTE

TIME REQUIRED
15-30 MINUTES

IN/OUTDOOR
IN OUT

ACTIVITY LEVEL

CLEANUP LEVEL

GROSS FACTOR

Circle Soccer

MATERIALS NEEDED

A large beach ball
A long rope

PREPARATION

Blow up the beach ball.

HOW TO PLAY

Divide students into two teams. Form a large circle with team members on the same side of a circle, then lay a rope down the center of the circle so team can tell what side they are on. Remind them that just like regular soccer, they cannot use their arms or hands to touch the ball. The object of the game is to try and kick the beach ball past (or over) the other team. The team members can do whatever they want to try and stop it, *except* use their arms and hands. This game moves fast. Give a point each time one team manages to get the ball past the other team. The first team to get 10 points wins.

Clothespin Connection

This is a wild and crazy game that gets the whole group involved.

MATERIALS NEEDED

Lots of spring-type clothespins (at least two per student)

HOW TO PLAY

Give each student two clothespins. On the word "go," they are to try and clip clothespins on the clothing of anyone else in the room. Instruct them to stop when you signal by yelling "Stop," blowing a whistle, etc.

Variation

The winner is the first one to get rid of his or her clothespins, but this can be boring as someone is likely to be pin-less in seconds. A better way to determine a winner is the person who has no pins when you yell, "Stop!" This may create numerous winners so you could have the "losers" sit down and have a play-off round.

SPECIAL FEATURES

NUMBER
15-50 PEOPLE

PREP TIME
NONE

TIME REQUIRED
5-10 MINUTES

IN/OUTDOOR
IN OUT

ACTIVITY LEVEL

CLEANUP LEVEL

GROSS FACTOR

SPECIAL FEATURES

NUMBER

12-30 PEOPLE

PREP TIME

5-10 MINUTES

TIME REQUIRED

15-30 MINUTES

IN/OUTDOOR

IN OUT

ACTIVITY LEVEL

CLEANUP LEVEL

GROSS FACTOR

Electric Fence

MATERIALS NEEDED

A sturdy rope at least 20 feet long
Two poles, trees or other sturdy stationary objects

PREPARATION

Tie a rope about five feet off the ground between two poles, trees or other sturdy structures. The ideal would be to use volleyball poles.

HOW TO PLAY

Divide the group into teams of 6 to 10 members each. The object is for everyone on the team to get over the "electric fence" without touching it. This is very similar to the kind of games seen in most ropes courses. Have teams do this one at a time. No one is allowed to go under or around the rope or to touch the poles or the rope.

If you want, you can give a team a point each time someone touches the rope. The team with the *least* number of points wins. Or you can just use this as a teamwork-building game.

Variation

Assign various "handicaps" to a few of the team members, such as "broken limbs," a blindfold to restrict sight, tying shoelaces together, etc. Use any idea you can to make the challenge more interesting and fun.

5/24/99

Fruit Basket

MATERIALS NEEDED

Enough chairs for everyone to be seated.

HOW TO PLAY

Have everyone arrange their chairs in a circle facing the middle. Have one student sit on a chair in the middle of the circle. Give everyone a name of a fruit, using only four fruits (i.e., bananas, apples, oranges and peaches). The person in the middle says "I want to eat a (name of one of the four fruits)." All of those fruits must then get up and run to another chair while the student who called out the fruit tries to get a chair too. The last student standing is now It. He or she sits down in the middle and calls a name of a fruit. Once in awhile It can yell "Fruit basket's upset!" and everyone gets up and runs for another chair.

Variations

- Use colors they are wearing: "I want to meet someone with blue on."
- Use animal names, Bible names, professional sports teams, etc.

SPECIAL FEATURES

NUMBER
15-50 PEOPLE

PREP TIME
NONE

TIME REQUIRED
10-20 MINUTES

INDOOR

ACTIVITY LEVEL

CLEANUP LEVEL

GROSS FACTOR

SPECIAL FEATURES

NUMBER

15-50 PEOPLE

PREP TIME

1-5 MINUTES

TIME REQUIRED

10-15 MINUTES

IN/OUTDOOR

IN OUT

ACTIVITY LEVEL

CLEANUP LEVEL

GROSS FACTOR

Fruit Relay

MATERIALS NEEDED

Apples (or other round fruit or vegetables such as oranges, grapefruits, onions, etc.), one for each team

HOW TO PLAY

Divide your group into equal teams. Have them line up one person behind the other and give the first person in each line an apple (or other fruit). The first person places the apple under his or her chin and, on the word "go," passes the apple to the next person's chin without using their hands. This continues all the way to the end of the line. First line to completely pass the fruit to the end of the line wins.

One suggestion for a little added surprise: use ice cold apples!

Frustration

This is an add-on to familiar simple games such as tag, relay races, etc.

MATERIALS NEEDED

Have on hand such things as rope, duct tape, pantyhose, bricks or other heavy things to carry, cloth strips, etc.

HOW TO PLAY

The object is to keep handicapping the game to make it more and more difficult to play.

As the game is played, keep adding on rules. For example, tell students that all players have to play with their hands tied together—or a water balloon tucked in their shirt or holding their left foot and hopping or whatever you can think of. Keep adding on until the game becomes impossible to play!

SPECIAL FEATURES

NUMBER
10-50 PEOPLE

PREP TIME
1-10 MINUTES

TIME REQUIRED
15-20 MINUTES

IN/OUTDOOR
IN OUT

ACTIVITY LEVEL

CLEANUP LEVEL

GROSS FACTOR

Get Lost!

MATERIALS NEEDED

3x5-inch index cards
Two baskets or similar containers
Approximately 2x2-inch squares of paper

PREPARATION

On separate 3x5-inch index cards, write the names of enough differ-ent locations around your church to accommodate the number of stu-dents attending the meeting. Anywhere that is allowable is valid—kitchen sink, boiler room door, pastor's study door, copy machine, men's room, pulpit, organ, etc. Place these cards in a basket or other container.

Prepare lots of 2x2-inch slips of paper with the following notations: *L* (for left), *R* (for right), *S* (for straight) and *180* (for reverse—or you can use *REV*). Make enough for each player to have five (if in a small church), eight (if in a larger church) or 10 (if in a really large church). Determine the number of moves it might take for students to get from their locations back to the youth room. Place these slips of paper in a second container.

HOW TO PLAY

Upon arrival each student draws one location slip. The location they select will be their starting point. Then each student draws the same number of slips of paper (5, 8 or 10 slips of paper, according to church size) and keeps them in the order they drew them.

Upon hearing the command, "Get lost!" the students go to their starting locations and see where their list of directional cues has them end up. They follow the directions as in the order they drew them.

For example: If Toni drew the choir loft as her starting location, and her five directions were *L, L, R, 180, S,* she would go from the choir loft in the direction of her choice. At the first intersecting corridor, doorway or other obstacle, she would turn *left,* then *left* again at the next oppor-tunity to turn. She'd turn *right* the next time, then she would *reverse* the next time and go *straight* the next time she came to an intersect-ing hall or room. If steps are encountered, treat them as a hall.

Please note: This is an imperfect game. Some of the directional choices will be impossible. If the students get stuck—as they often do—they may skip the card on top for the next one, putting the unused card on the bottom for the last direction. Trust the students to make the appropriate adjustments as they encounter dead ends. Some students will find they can go almost nowhere. That's part of the game.

On rare occasions, someone's directions will actually lead them back to the meeting point. Award that person a cheap compass *after* you check their directions.

The game can have a significant teaching lead-in for lessons about following God's direction, or leading, in life. It points out that much of life comes to us unexpected, or that we can make wrong turns that take us away from our goals rather than toward them.

Gurning Contest

SPECIAL FEATURES

NUMBER
5+ PEOPLE

PREP TIME
60 MINUTES

TIME REQUIRED
15-30 MINUTES

INDOOR

ACTIVITY LEVEL

CLEANUP LEVEL

GROSS FACTOR

MATERIALS NEEDED

Camera
Slide film
Slide projector and screen

PREPARATION

This contest begins one week and concludes the following. It's a great way to build attendance and get students to come back! Provide a worthy prize (dinner for two, free movie passes, etc.) and tell everyone they have a chance to win. During free time or after your meeting when students are hanging out, pull individuals aside and take their picture. Now, this is no ordinary picture. They are to "gurn." What is a gurn? A gurn is the weirdest, craziest, goofiest face they can make. Snap their picture using slide film, then have the film developed during the week.

HOW TO PLAY

Show the slides to the whole group the next week. Have the entire group vote for the best gurner.

Tip: Have the slides enlarged into poster-size pictures for the youth room. When students graduate, give them their poster as a going-away present.

Hot Streak

MATERIALS NEEDED

TABOO - 8/98

3x5-inch index cards
Two stopwatches or watches with seconds indicators

PREPARATION

Write four words on each card. These can be four random words, or you can choose words related to a Bible study, retreat or meeting theme. Or you could use the key words in a Bible passage. Each list should have different, but related words, with increasing degrees of difficulty.

HOW TO PLAY

Divide the group into two teams. Ask for two volunteers from each team. Give each volunteer a card with the four words written on it. They are to describe each word in turn for their group without using the word. Their group members must try to guess what word they are trying to describe. For example: Let's say the first word is "bear." The volunteer might say, "It's a four-legged large furry animal that lives in the woods and it sounds like this 'Grrrr.'" They can use body language as well as words, but they cannot use the word on the list or any form of it. Have adult leaders time each team and the team to guess all four words the quickest wins!

SPECIAL FEATURES

NUMBER
10-50 PEOPLE

PREP TIME
15-30 MINUTES

TIME REQUIRED
15-30 MINUTES

INDOOR
IN

ACTIVITY LEVEL

CLEANUP LEVEL

GROSS FACTOR

SPECIAL FEATURES

NUMBER
20 PEOPLE

PREP TIME
10 MINUTES

TIME REQUIRED
30 MINUTES

INDOOR
IN

ACTIVITY LEVEL

CLEANUP LEVEL

GROSS FACTOR

REQUIREMENTS

Human Foosball

PLAYING AREA

Medium-sized room with four walls—the larger the group, the larger the room needed. However, stay somewhat confined. It is also important that the room be emptied of extra furniture to prevent accidents.

MATERIALS NEEDED

A Nerf ball
One chair for each player
Two small portable hockey/soccer nets for goals, or four cones or four chairs

PLAY AREA SETUP

The chairs should be arranged in the room using the same format as a foosball table.

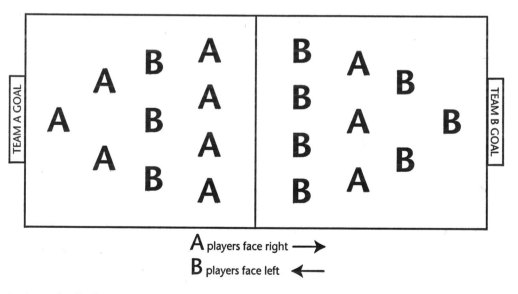

A players face right ⟶
B players face left ⟵

In Foosball the teams reflect their configurations as in a mirror, with a center line in between to divide the team sides. Against the back wall, guarding the goal area, is a goalie (Team A) whose chair stands between the two goal ends. In front of the goalie, place two defenders (Team A) who are stationed in front of the two goal side edges, but a good six or eight feet up from the sides. The next row is three members of the opposing team facing the defenders (Team B). The next

row closest to the center line, there are four more defenders (Team A).

The same setup applies for the opposing side. Goalie B, two goal defenders from B, a row of three Team A offensive players, and up on the center line a row of four more Team B players.

Adjust the chairs to fit the room. Each game will accommodate 20 players total—10 for each team. If your youth group is larger than 20, you can rotate players or whole teams, or if space allows, play two games simultaneously.

HOW TO PLAY

Play the game the same as Foosball (or soccer), except that each student sits in a chair. They may swivel their bodies around on their chairs, but they cannot lift their bodies from the chair at anytime. They may only touch the ball with their feet. Advisors may need to be ready to retrieve balls that cannot be played.

Scoring is one point per goal, or why not award a million points per goal!

The ball may be bounced off the walls when being passed. If it stops in an area where no players can reach it without leaving their seats, either have an advisor grab it and lob it back into the play area, or call out "Up for grabs!" and designate which two of the closest students can scramble for it. These two "scramblers" cannot play it until they are once again seated.

SPECIAL FEATURES

NUMBER
15-50 PEOPLE

PREP TIME
5 MINUTES

TIME REQUIRED
15 MINUTES

INDOOR

ACTIVITY LEVEL

CLEANUP LEVEL

GROSS FACTOR

Indoor Scavenger Hunt

PREPARATION

Prepare a list of about ten items that can be found inside the meeting room and preferably within the team itself. Some examples include: a credit card, a shiny penny, a blonde hair, school ID, driver's license, a note from school, picture of family, etc.

HOW TO PLAY

Divide the group into teams. Stand in the middle of the room and have the teams sit in groups circled around you. Call out the name of an object to be found. The teams search within the group or they may send out one student to find the object within the room. The first person on a team to bring that object to the leader earns points for his or her team. The team with the most points wins.

Kitchen Olympics

PREPARATION

Get permission to use the church kitchen.

If permission is not granted to use the church kitchen, you could let the groups choose from a table of items that you have gathered from the kitchen or other source. Provide a wide variety of objects so that each team has a choice of items.

HOW TO PLAY

At the beginning of the meeting, divide students into groups representing countries. They may choose from a list of presently existing countries, or invent a country of their own.

Their task is to develop a Kitchen Olympic event that they will teach, lead and compete in. Each event needs to include some aspect of the kitchen, whether a utensil, food item or whatever. (If food is available for their selection, either play outside or cover the floors of the meeting room with plastic.)

The challenge is for each country team to introduce and teach its event, then have all of the teams compete against one another. The adult advisors will be the judges.

Award prizes, ribbons or medals for winners, or announce that everyone is a winner and serve a dessert or other treat.

A few event suggestions for the Kitchen Olympics events include:

Javelin throw for distance (using toothpicks or strands of spaghetti)
Egg tossing (either how far or who can toss back and forth without breaking it)
Find the penny in the bowl of flour (using only one hand, reach into the flour and try to grab the hidden penny, one chance per contestant)
Soup-can bowling (roll soup cans to knock down "pins"— paper cups)
Marshmallow stuffing (score most marshmallows held in mouth at one time)

Encourage their creativity in thinking of their own events.

SPECIAL FEATURES

NUMBER
15-50 PEOPLE

PREP TIME
10-15 MINUTES

TIME REQUIRED
30-60 MINUTES

IN/OUTDOOR
IN OUT

ACTIVITY LEVEL

CLEANUP LEVEL

GROSS FACTOR

Group Games

Kool Aid Relay

This is a fun relay that involves everyone and is particularly fun to observe!

MATERIALS NEEDED

Several packages of the same flavor *unsweetened* Kool Aid
Enough straws for each player to have one
Plastic drinking glasses, two for each team
One or two long tables (depending on the number of teams)

PREPARATION

Prepare a pitcherful of Kool Aid using several packages instead of one and no sugar so that mixture is super-strong and super-sour. Set up table(s) at the front of the playing area.

HOW TO PLAY

Divide the group into three to six teams (depending on the size of your group) and have them line up one team member behind the other. Set a large glass (one for each team) filled with Kool Aid on the table(s) 50 or so feet away from where the teams are lined up. Also, set an empty glass next to each filled glass. Give each member on each team a straw. The object of this game is for students, one at a time, to run to the glass with the Kool Aid, sip some of the Kool Aid through the straw and then spit it back into the empty glass. The team that puts the greatest amount of Kool Aid into the glass within a certain amount of time wins. Or after everyone has had one turn, determine the winner by which team has the most Kool Aid in its glass.

The fun part of this game is that the Kool Aid is super strong (one recipe made with several packages) and unsweetened. The students will think that they are going to drink this sweet liquid and get quite a shock when they taste this super-duper bitter, tart and tangy mixture! The results are hilarious.

SPECIAL FEATURES

NUMBER
15-50 PEOPLE

PREP TIME
10-15 MINUTES

TIME REQUIRED
15-30 MINUTES

IN/OUTDOOR
IN OUT

ACTIVITY LEVEL

CLEANUP LEVEL

GROSS FACTOR

Variation

Prepare more of the super-strong, super-sour Kool Aid mixture, but give each student a paper cup and straw of their own and have them race to see who is the first to transfer their Kool Aid into another paper cup.

SPECIAL FEATURES

NUMBER

12-15 PEOPLE

PREP TIME

20 MINUTES

TIME REQUIRED

30-45 MINUTES

INDOOR

ACTIVITY LEVEL

CLEANUP LEVEL

GROSS FACTOR

REQUIREMENTS

Long Travel Games

The following games are lifesavers on longer trips when the fun of riding in a van or bus begins to wear off. The games can be adapted for use on a large bus, but are explained here for use in large 12 to 15-passenger vans.

License Plate Scrabble

MATERIALS NEEDED

> Several 3x5-inch index cards
> Hundreds of small square slips of paper
> Two rolls of masking or transparent tape
> Felt-tip pens

PREPARATION

On several of the square slips of paper, write individual letters to provide "supply letters" for the teams to draw from, but leave most of the slips blank. For supply letters, provide several with the vowels written on them and several with the most commonly used consonants. A regular Scrabble game can give you guidelines.

HOW TO PLAY

Many, if not most states have letters on the license plates for passenger cars. In this game you divide the passengers into two even teams, the front seats versus the back seats. Give each team several 3x5-inch index cards.

Each team has three kinds of workers: the Spotters, who locate and call out the letters on car plates; the Scribes, who jot the letters of plates onto slips of paper; and the Spellers, who take the letters written on the slips, then create words out of the letters using the collected letters and the "supply letters" that they draw at the beginning of the game.

The game proceeds in this way: Each team draws one letter per person on their team. So, if there are six students per team, each team receives six letters. This is their supply. The supply is given to the

Spellers who may wish to tape them on a seat for easy viewing. The Scribes (one or two are needed) are supplied with lots of slips of paper and a felt-tip pen each. The Spotters need to be located next to a window where they can easily see the passing traffic.

As a car comes into view, a Spotter calls out the letters seen on the license plate to the team Scribe. The Scribe records the letters on slips of paper and hands them to the Speller. The Spellers must then use the letters, plus up to two letters from their supply to create words. They must use all of the available letters and no more than two additional letters. They may rearrange the letters in anyway they choose, but complete words have to be created. The words are then written on the index cards. Once a supply letter is used, it cannot be used again. When a team has used its entire stock of supply letters, it may draw six more.

The game is scored by counting the most words each team creates.

SPECIAL FEATURES

NUMBER

5+ PEOPLE

PREP TIME

NONE

TIME REQUIRED

N/A

INDOOR

IN

ACTIVITY LEVEL

CLEANUP LEVEL

GROSS FACTOR

REQUIREMENTS

Stupid Sign Spotting Contest

MATERIALS NEEDED

Paper
Pens or pencils

Challenge the students to keep track of ridiculously worded signs along the way. Misspellings, bizarre claims or ads, announcements and the like are all fair game. Have students write down what they see so that they can share them later. Or have a group scribe record everyone's sightings, then read your collection at the end of the day or at the end of the trip. Have students vote for the stupidest or funniest.

Incidentally, these signs can become trip slogans in no time.

Travel Scavenger Hunt

Since the invention of cars, we have played games using car makes or models as symbols. In the 60s VW Bugs were known as "punch buggies" or "slugbugs" because the person spotting a VW and calling out its name had permission to give a good-natured punch in the arm to another person as a reward. Similar recognition penalties were linked to other cars as well, such as "Corvair, pull your hair."

While Corvairs are nearly extinct and VW Bugs are becoming rare, there is the potential for a world of new innovations surrounding names or nicknames of various vehicles.

MATERIALS NEEDED

> Photocopies of grid page
> Pens or pencils

PREPARATION

Using the following list, prepare a grid sheet similar to the sample on page 58:

- Winks—cars with broken or burned-out brake or rear lights
- Popeyes—cars with one headlight burned out
- Police cars
- Ambulances
- Tow trucks
- Breakdowns
- Trucks that sound their air horns
- Cars with ski or bike racks
- Junkers

How to Play

Travel Scavenger Hunts can be informal or formal. The informal game is when the spotted car is linked to some phrase or behavior that is then acted out. However, the whole thing can become a more formal competition if you plan ahead and prepare a grid on a sheet of paper for keeping records.

When the game becomes boring, call a break until an agreed-upon time, then resume. When a vehicle is spotted, it should be called out and identified. First caller gets the point. Most points accumulated at the end of the trip wins.

SPECIAL FEATURES

NUMBER
5+ PEOPLE

PREP TIME
10 MINUTES

TIME REQUIRED
N/A

INDOOR
IN

ACTIVITY LEVEL

CLEANUP LEVEL

GROSS FACTOR

REQUIREMENTS

A Sample Grid

Winks	Popeyes	Police Cars
Tow Trucks	Breakdowns	Air Horn Blasts
Ambulances	Ski or Bike Racks	Junkers

PREDICTIONS COMPETITION

PREPARATION

Before a long trip, challenge the students to establish a number of predictions of happenings that will probably occur on the trip. Set several things that can be predicted and let the students each have one guess for each prediction. Record these guesses on a chart and assign someone to keep track of the numbers.

Some sample predictions:

- Time of arrival at destination
- Length of the trip, in minutes
- Miles traveled
- Total number of gas fill-ups needed
- Total number of potty stops
- First person to complain
- Who will get car sick
- First person to fall asleep
- First thing to be spilled
- Number of traffic jams

Other suggested predictions can be to guess what type of gas station will be the tenth one passed on the trip or which fast food restaurant will be the twenty-first passed, and so on.

HOW TO PLAY

Have your recorder write down the statistics as they occur. Give points for each correct guess. The highest score wins. These need to be confined to highway driving for easy tabulating. Trying to keep track in a business district is pretty frustrating.

SPECIAL NOTE

For travel game winners, have prizes or awards that reflect the trip. Gather trip memorabilia such as maps, car trash bags, restaurant napkins, change found in the vehicle, car cups, toll or gasoline receipts, pebbles, shells, seeds, etc.—anything that can be collected along the way.

SPECIAL FEATURES

NUMBER
5+ PEOPLE

PREP TIME
10 MINUTES

TIME REQUIRED
N/A

INDOOR
IN

ACTIVITY LEVEL

CLEANUP LEVEL

GROSS FACTOR

REQUIREMENTS

SPECIAL FEATURES

NUMBER
15-50 PEOPLE

PREP TIME
10 MINUTES

TIME REQUIRED
15-30 MINUTES

INDOOR
IN

ACTIVITY LEVEL

CLEANUP LEVEL

GROSS FACTOR

Magazine Find

MATERIALS NEEDED

Four identical magazines

PREPARATION

Scan the magazines ahead of time and choose about 10 items that the teams will later have to find in the magazine. Make a list of specific pictures, headlines, advertisements, etc. Jot down the page numbers in case you stump them and you need to show that the item is really there.

HOW TO PLAY

Divide the group into four teams and have them gather one team in each of the four corners of the playing area. Call out the items one at a time. When a team finds the called item, they must rip it out and bring it to you or another designated leader. The first team to do so receives 50 points. The team that gets the most points wins!

Mirror Maze Challenge

SPECIAL FEATURES

NUMBER
15-50 PEOPLE

PREP TIME
30-60 MINUTES

TIME REQUIRED
30-60 MINUTES

INDOOR

ACTIVITY LEVEL

CLEANUP LEVEL

GROSS FACTOR

MATERIALS NEEDED

Two large mirrors
Chairs and/or large pieces of cardboard

PREPARATION

Use large hand mirrors or prepare one-foot square mirror tiles by applying tape around the edges—to avoid cuts. Set up a maze using folding chairs and/or cardboard, or whatever you can find to make the dividers. To avoid injuries the maze corridors should be wide enough for two people to pass one another.

HOW TO PLAY

The object of the game is to walk through the maze by looking into a mirror that is held out perpendicular to the forehead just above the eyebrows. The reflecting surface points downward toward the feet. To maneuver, the player has to look up into the mirror to see where he or she is walking.

Divide students into teams, or you can use this as a challenge between two group members. Two students will try to navigate through the maze at the same time. If you have more than two teams, you can time each person and the one with the best time wins.

Scoring is kept by giving a point for each time a participant touches the chairs or other barricades. The object is to get the lowest number of points. Also, give points if the participant looks around and does not use the mirror continually as the viewing point. You can also keep track of the time it takes to move through the maze. Award the fastest time with least amount of points.

SPECIAL FEATURES

NUMBER
15-50 PEOPLE

PREP TIME
15-30 MINUTES

TIME REQUIRED
20 MINUTES

OUTDOOR
OUT

ACTIVITY LEVEL

CLEANUP LEVEL

GROSS FACTOR

Nickname Spud

Spud, that longtime staple of youth group ball games, can be adapted in a hilarious way by assigning each teenager a nickname before the game instead of the usual number.

MATERIALS NEEDED

> Several sheets of poster board or newsprint (or at least two portable white boards)
> One large rubber playground ball
> Name tags (or slips of papers cut the size of name tags)

PREPARATION

Make a list of a number of nicknames equal to the number of players. Write the names in big letters on large sheets of posterboards or newsprint (or on at least two portable white boards) and display them around the playing area so they can be easily seen.

HOW TO PLAY

As players arrive, give each of them a nickname on a name tag or slip of paper. Instruct them to keep their tags in their pockets for future reference. Some will have trouble remembering the name, as they will be new to them and they might have to refer to their name tags to remind themselves.

Have students play Spud by calling the nicknames from the posters or white boards. Spud is played outdoors. Everyone is bunched together in the playing area. One person is selected to be It. The person who is It is given the ball, and then calls a nickname as he or she throws the ball into the air. While the ball is in the air, everyone runs away from It. The person whose nickname is called is now It and he or she has to catch or pick up the ball. When the new It has the ball, he or she yells, "Spud!" When Spud is called, everyone must immediately stop where they are. It then may take three steps toward any player and throw the ball to try and hit that player. If the ball is caught by the player or misses the player completely, It remains It. If the player is hit

by the ball and it bounces off, then the player becomes the new It. The game continues in this way.

There is no winner in this game. Just play for a certain amount of time or until students begin to get bored.

Variation: Characteristic Spud

The person holding the ball calls an identifying characteristic of the particular player they want to be It. For example, if Tom wants to call Janice, he must call her by shouting something about her that everyone knows. Maybe it's the color of her T-shirt, the model of her car, her shoe brand, her favorite activity, an instrument she plays, whatever. They must think of an identifying characteristic that everyone will recognize. It will cause confusion if the same characteristic is shared by others.

The Pantyhose Event

This requires lots of pantyhose. You could ask church members to donate old pantyhose for these activities. What a great way to encourage recycling!

MATERIALS NEEDED

LOTS of pantyhose
Several pairs of mittens (one pair for each team)
Tennis balls—two per team
Several water balloons

BEFORE YOU BEGIN

Divide the whole group into fairly equal teams of five to eight members per team. Be sure you have enough materials to allow full participation for the number of teams you have formed. Some of the games require only one representative from each team while others require participation of every team member.

These games would be great as part of an all-nighter or retreat.

Three-Legged Pantyhose Race

Have students remove their shoes for ease in putting the pantyhose on and off. Two people on each team put on a pair of pantyhose, each using one of the available legs, creating a three-legged situation. When everyone is properly garbed, have a three-legged race, or a three-legged relay race, between the teams. To make the race even more interesting create an obstacle course for participants to race through.

Pantyhose with Mittens

Have each team choose a player to represent its team. Give each player a pair of mittens and a pair of pantyhose. The object is to put the pantyhose on the quickest over shoes, pants, etc., with the mittens covering the hands.

This could also be done in the form of a relay, having each team member race to put the pantyhose on and take them off, then hand it off to the next team member until every member has put on and taken off the pantyhose.

Pantyhose Putt

Divide each team in half and line up one-half of each team on one side of the playing area and the other half on the other side, having the first person in each half facing each other with the other team members lined up behind them. Each team is given a pair of pantyhose with a tennis ball in the toe of one of the legs. Each relay participant is to tie the empty leg of the pantyhose around his or her waist so that the tennis ball hangs behind their backs and between their legs. The object is to swing the tennis ball in the pantyhose leg back and forth to "putt" (hit) a second tennis ball along the ground across the playing area where a switch is made with the next player who ties the pantyhose around his or her waist, and then putts the tennis ball on the ground back to the third player. This continues until each member of each team has had a turn.

Think of the putt as similar to the croquet putt where the mallet is sometimes swung between the legs only you do not use your hands. A flat, hard surface makes the best playing field. This works well inside or on a parking lot. This is a challenging game; it could even be called difficult, but it is a blast to play and even more fun to watch.

Samurai Water Balloon Fight

Choose one participant from each team. For each team prepare a pair of pantyhose with a water balloon in one of the legs. Each participant then puts the elastic waist of a pair of pantyhose on his or her head. At your signal play begins as students swing the balloons around their heads and attempt to break them against the bodies of their opponents. Play continues until all water balloons are broken. The driest person wins for his or her team.

SPECIAL
FEATURES

NUMBER

12-32 PEOPLE

PREP TIME

45 MINUTES

TIME REQUIRED

30 MINUTES

IN/OUTDOOR

IN OUT

ACTIVITY LEVEL

CLEANUP LEVEL

GROSS FACTOR

Paper Plane Puzzle Contest

MATERIALS NEEDED

Four easy puzzles of 35 to 50 pieces
Lots of 8½x11-inch paper scratch paper (recycle old handouts, etc.)
Four different colors of felt-tip pens
Four sheets of different colored construction paper, the same colors as the felt-tip pens
Transparent or masking tape
Four containers (the bottoms of the puzzle boxes work fine)

PREPARATION

It's important that the four puzzles be very different, but have the same size and number of pieces. Don't get really large puzzles, nor any that are too small. Open each of the puzzle boxes. Using a different color of felt-tip pen for each puzzle, mark each piece on the back with a large spot. Mark all pieces of the first puzzle with one color, the second puzzle with another, and so on until each piece in each puzzle is marked. Divide the number of puzzle pieces into fourths and put one-quarter of each puzzle into each of the four containers. Each container will hold one quarter of each of the puzzles. Each will contain enough pieces to make one puzzle. Mark each container using one of the four colors that you used to mark the backs of the pieces. Tape one of each of the four sheets of colored construction paper corresponding to the puzzles to a different corner of the room.

HOW TO PLAY

When the students arrive, divide them into four teams of approximately equal size. Assign one of the four colors to each team, i.e., there might be a Red Team, Green Team, Blue Team and Orange Team. Give each team the puzzle container that is marked with its color. Then have the teams find the corner of the meeting room that has their color of paper attached to the wall. Each team will also need to be given a large stack of 8½x11-inch paper.

Give the following directions: "This contest requires your team to

successfully put together a puzzle. However, you only have one quarter of your puzzle in your container. The other teams around the room each have one quarter of your puzzle. So, the object is to get your puzzle pieces from the other groups and to get their pieces to them, as well. However, you may not simply walk over and deliver the pieces. Instead, you have to build paper planes and fly the pieces to its home group. The first team to successfully build their puzzle wins."

It is wise to assign an adult leader to each group to insure that they do fly the pieces to their destinations. Also, one or two adults will be needed to patrol the center of the room for planes and pieces that do not make it to their destinations. These can be returned to any of the groups, equally distributing them, to groups other than their color destination for "reflying." The first team to put together its puzzle completely (and "flown" all the other puzzle pieces to the other teams) is the winner.

SPECIAL FEATURES

NUMBER
10-30 PEOPLE

PREP TIME
10-20 MINUTES

TIME REQUIRED
5-10 MINUTES

INDOOR

ACTIVITY LEVEL

CLEANUP LEVEL

GROSS FACTOR

Ping-Pong Launch

MATERIALS NEEDED

Lots of ping-pong balls
Lots of plastic spoons
One two-liter soda bottle for each team

PREPARATION

Cut the neck off the two-liter soda bottles.

HOW TO PLAY

The object of the game is for each team to try to launch ping-pong balls across the room and into their soda bottles.

Divide the group into teams, making sure you have enough soda bottles so that each team has its own. Line bottles up against a wall. Line teams up a set distance away from their bottles. (You may want to experiment with the distance before playing the game.) The players on each team are each given a ping-pong ball and a plastic spoon. They are to hold the spoon with the handle pointing away from them and toward the bottle. They place the ping-pong balls in their spoons and while holding the spoon handles in one hand, they pull back the top of their spoons and the balls with the other hand as one would a catapult. They then release the tops of the spoons (while continuing to hold the handles) and the balls, launching them in an attempt to drop it into the soda bottle. If they hit the shot, the ping-pong ball drops through.

This can be played with everyone on the team shooting at once, or by lining the students up and everyone shooting at once. When all of the ping-pong balls have been launched, collect each team's bottle and count the number of "bull's-eyes" each team got.

Recycling Sculptures

This is more of an activity, but it also has a competition element that makes it a fun group event. It will take about an hour and a half to complete. This could also be a great activity for an all-nighter or retreat.

SEVERAL WEEKS BEFORE
For several weeks before the event, solicit students and the congregation to bring in lots of recyclable materials such as aluminum cans, plastic bottles, cereal and oatmeal boxes, newspapers, cardboard, Styrofoam packing materials and meat trays, etc. Collect these in large plastic trash bags.

MATERIALS NEEDED

    Recycled materials
    Several Bibles
    Several rolls of masking/duct tape
    Utility knives and scissors
    String
    Wire
    Heavy duty glue and/or hot glue guns
    And various other fasteners

PREPARATION
On the day of the event, dump the contents of all the bags out together, creating one big heap. The middle of a parking lot is great. If you are using a large room (and you'll need a large room if you do this inside), be sure to put down a tarp or sheet of plastic in case the containers were not properly rinsed out. You don't want soda stains on the carpet!

HOW TO PLAY
When the students gather, divide them into teams of approximately five to eight members each. The teams are then assigned with the task of creating the most understandable interpretation of a Bible story, parable or Bible verse. They could select their own (but they must keep

SPECIAL FEATURES

NUMBER
10-100 PEOPLE

PREP TIME
15 MINUTES

TIME REQUIRED
60-90 MINUTES

IN/OUTDOOR
IN OUT

ACTIVITY LEVEL

CLEANUP LEVEL

GROSS FACTOR

REQUIREMENTS

it to themselves) or you could prepare some on small slips of paper ahead of time for them to draw from.

After choosing their story or passage, have them gather supplies, spread out (around the large area or in separate rooms or designated outdoor areas) and begin to create. Give them a time limit to complete their sculptures.

After the time is up, have them bring their sculpture back to the main meeting area. Have the other teams guess each team's story or Scripture passage.

Don't award a prize for the best or most realistic. Let them stand on their own merit, congratulating the students on their team efforts, not on the final project.

If you really want to give out awards, give an award to each team, such as Most Imaginative, Best Use of Supplies, Most Difficult, Best Choice of Scripture, Largest, Smallest, Most Likely to Operate on Its Own, etc.

Clean up by hauling the whole mess to the recycle center or to the trash bins, then reward the whole group with an edible treat.

Seated Hide 'n' Seek

MATERIALS NEEDED

A chair
A blindfold
Small slips of paper
A black felt-tip pen
A metal pie pan
An empty soda bottle
A sign designating North

PREPARATION

Play this version of Hide 'n' Seek in a park or other outdoor, wooded area with lots of natural cover. You will need a chair, a blindfold, a container with many slips of paper on which numerous step amounts (i.e., 1 step, 2 steps, 3 steps, 4 steps, and so on up to 10) are written. Make a spinner by drawing lines of the eight compass directions on a round metal pie pan. Use a soda bottle as your spinner. You also need to designate where north is in the playing area.

HOW TO PLAY

Set a chair in the middle of a large, wooded play area. Instruct the students that the person in the chair will be It. He or she will be blindfolded. As It is counting to 100, the students scurry off and hide in all directions around the area. Designate what distance (in steps) is the limit for the game.

After everyone has hidden and It reaches 100, remove the blindfold. Have It spin for the direction, then draw a step card from the container. Replace the blindfold and lead It in the direction of the spin, counting out the number of steps that was on the slip of paper he or she drew from the container. The person leading It needs to be fair and not allow It to walk into trees or trip over things. If the steps are obstructed by a tree or other obstacle, the assistant leads It around the tree and continues in the correct direction.

SPECIAL FEATURES

NUMBER
15-50 PEOPLE

PREP TIME
20 MINUTES

TIME REQUIRED
30-60 MINUTES

OUTDOOR

ACTIVITY LEVEL

CLEANUP LEVEL

GROSS FACTOR

Upon reaching the point that the number of steps takes It, he or she removes the blindfold and "catches" the first person he or she sees. This person is now It. If no one is in sight, It spins again, draws another slip of paper and is blindfolded again.

Note: It's important that those who are hiding do not move around or change hiding places. Once they hide, they have to stay put. Some students might hide in front of a tree, assuming that It will walk beyond them and the tree will then become cover. Others might hide behind a tree and be unhidden as It walks past them. The students should be instructed to be partially in sight. Some will want to cover themselves with leaves or lie down in low spots or under bushes. Make a rule that they can only get down as low as sitting or kneeling. The game is no fun if It cannot see anyone to call out.

Variations

1. Continue play from the point of the first "find," blindfolding the one just caught and spinning from that point, walking the number of steps on the slip of paper from that point. If this option is used, a second assistant will be needed to move the chair, compass and steps container to the point of play.

2. Always return to the original point, calling "all in free," then starting over with the first one caught now becoming It.

3. Play elimination and allow It to call out all of the people he or she sees from the destination point. Everyone else remains hidden. The first one found becomes It, returns to the chair, takes his or her turn and eliminates more from the new area of play that the designated steps and direction takes him or her.

Servant Scavenger Hunt

OBJECT OF THE GAME

This is a scavenger hunt with great community public relations and mission experiences. Small groups of four to five students go into the community or to the homes and businesses of the church members and do service activities in the home or business for points. At the end they return to the church and share their experiences.

PREPARATION

Prepare a sheet similar to the following sample score sheet. Make enough copies for each team to have a copy. Also, give each team a pen for gathering the signatures. Assign one adult to each team of students.

Sample Score Sheet

Servant Scavenger Hunt Record Sheet

Project	Point Value	Signature of Recipient
1. Mow one lawn	1000	_____
2. Sweep three driveways	200 each	_____
3. Empty four wastebaskets	100 each	_____
4. Wash one car	500	_____
5. Sweep one garage	350	_____
6. Vacuum one living room	300	_____
7. Change one light bulb	100	_____
8. Dust the living room furniture	200	_____
9. Water two plants	250	_____
10. Vacuum the inside of one car	300	_____
11. Walk a dog around the block	400	_____
12. Clean a mirror	200	_____
13. Play ball with some kids	500	_____
Total Points earned	_____	

Time your group returned _____
Checked by _____

SPECIAL FEATURES

NUMBER
10-100 PEOPLE

PREP TIME
15 MINUTES

TIME REQUIRED
90 MINUTES

OUTDOOR

ACTIVITY LEVEL

CLEANUP LEVEL

GROSS FACTOR

REQUIREMENTS

HOW TO PLAY

Time Limit: 1 hour, 30 minutes.

Teams may not do more than two projects at one home or business. Also they are not allowed to take any money for the work they do. This is a service project for the community (or church family). The winning team is the one that has the most points at the end of the time limit.

This activity is a wonderful way to promote Christian service while letting your community know that your group is active and visible. Close with a prayer circle thanking God that your group is located in a town that can be influenced by simple acts of love.

Shoe Relay

The more students you have for this relay, the better!

PREPARATION
Have everyone take off their shoes and throw them into a pile in the middle of the playing area. Have a leader mix up the pile of shoes.

HOW TO PLAY
Divide the group into equal teams of four to six members each. Have them line up in their teams facing the pile of shoes. When you give the signal to go, first members on each team run to the pile of shoes. Each one finds his or her own shoes, puts them on, ties them and then returns to his or her team. Then the next team member runs to the pile, finds his or her own shoes and puts them on. This continues until each team member has found and put on his or her shoes. First team finished wins.

SPECIAL FEATURES

NUMBER
15-50 PEOPLE

PREP TIME
NONE

TIME REQUIRED
10-20 MINUTES

IN/OUTDOOR
IN OUT

ACTIVITY LEVEL

CLEANUP LEVEL

GROSS FACTOR

SPECIAL FEATURES

NUMBER
10-100 PEOPLE

PREP TIME
10 MINUTES

TIME REQUIRED
30-40 MINUTES

OUTDOOR
OUT

ACTIVITY LEVEL

CLEANUP LEVEL

GROSS FACTOR

Signs of Nature Scavenger Hunt

This game can be played close to home, on a picnic, at a retreat, campout or church camp.

MATERIALS NEEDED

A grocery bag for each team
Pens or pencils
Paper

Divide students into groups of six to eight members. Assign an adult to each group. Give each group a pen or pencil, paper and a grocery bag, then send them on a signs-of-nature scavenger hunt. The object of the game is to collect or record as many signs of nature as possible in a given time period. Give them a definite time period, say 30 to 40 minutes, to complete their hunt.

If the items they spot are collectible, they should put the objects in their bag. If not, they must have an adult advisor note it on paper. Due to the usual high level of competitiveness among students, it is advisable that an adult go with each group to rule on what is collectible and what is not. Also, one team might claim to have seen a herd of giraffes or an elephant track.

They can collect any sign of nature. They can collect feathers, egg shells, mouse bedding, spider webs, broken seeds and nuts, abandoned nests, fallen leaves, etc. They should record things such as animal droppings, tracks, animals sightings, etc. The group with the most accumulated sightings and physical evidence wins.

"Sit Down If..."

PREPARATION

Design your own personal "Sit down if..." list with personal references to your group. Begin the list with more general statements and gradually get more detailed. For example, tell the students "Sit down if..."

- You aren't wearing deodorant tonight.
- Your mom's name is Thelma.
- You sniff army boots.
- You were born in Alaska.
- You ate ham tonight.
- You've got a Michael Jackson poster in your room.
- You puked this month.
- You've ever dated Susie.
- You are wearing a red shirt.
- Anyone in this room has kissed you.

Toward the end of the game you might have to ad lib the last few statements to eliminate the last few students.

HOW TO PLAY

Have everyone stand up in front of their chairs. Tell them that you are going to read a list beginning with the phrase "Sit down if..." If the phrase honestly describes them, they are out of the game and they must sit down. The last person left standing wins!

SPECIAL FEATURES

NUMBER
15-100 PEOPLE

PREP TIME
5 MINUTES

TIME REQUIRED
5-10 MINUTES

IN/OUTDOOR

ACTIVITY LEVEL

CLEANUP LEVEL

GROSS FACTOR

Spin-the-Chair Name Game

This works well as a means to involve the youth group in learning the names of new students. However, don't use it too soon in the new year because the students need to know some of the names of the newer students. Wait until a month or so into the new program year.

MATERIALS NEEDED

A swivel chair
A red and a blue felt-tip pen

PREPARATION

Have students form a circle. They can be sitting on the floor or in chairs. Place the swivel chair in the center of the circle. Walk around the circle and alternately mark one hand of every other student with either a red dot or a blue dot. Tell students that the color on their hands designates which team they are on—the Red Team or the Blue Team.

HOW TO PLAY

Choose one student to sit in the swivel chair in the center of the circle. Have the student in the chair close his or her eyes and point straight ahead with one hand. Give him or her a good spin and when the spinning stops, the student opens his or her eyes and names the person that he or she is pointing at. If the circle is large, you may need to use a yardstick as a pointer that is held in one hand of the student being spun. If the identification is correct, the student in the chair trades places with the student he or she correctly named. If the identification is incorrect, he or she stays in the chair and continues to try to identify the other students until he or she is correct.

Scoring can be done in two ways. One is to make it an all-group game (this works best for smaller groups) and have the students marked off with a red or blue dot on the back of their hand for team identification. The students should alternate red, blue, red, blue

As a reminder to youth leaders: please exercise due caution when using games, crowdbreakers and community builders that are high activity or involve food. Gospel Light cannot be held responsible for any injuries incurred.

around the circle. Scoring is done when the student being identified is named by the student in the chair. If the person in the chair is correct, his or her team gets the point. If he or she gives an incorrect name, then the person who is incorrectly named gets to be It and sit in the chair.

Option for a large group: The Blue Team and the Red Team compete separately, forming separate circles with their own teammates. The Blue Team gets points for correct identifications made by the person in the chair in their circle, and the Red Team does the same. Have adult leaders keep score for each team. The team with the most points at the end of the allotted rounds is the winner because their team knew more of the group members' names than did the other team.

Tip: Adult leaders need to supervise the game to make sure that name leaks are not whispered. Also, don't let the students know they will be playing a name game beforehand, or they might try at the last minute to memorize the names of the new students.

Steal the Bacon Plus

These are suggested variations on this well-known game.

MATERIALS NEEDED

An object to be "stolen" (a block of wood, piece of cloth, etc.)
See the Variations section for added materials needed

HOW TO PLAY

The traditional way to play the game: First, divide your group into two teams, and have the teams line up on opposite sides of the playing area, facing each other. Give each student on one team a number, then number the students on the other team with the same numbers.

Place an object (a block of wood, a piece of cloth, etc.) in the middle of the room and call out a number. The two students who have the same number, one from each team, will race to the middle to try to grab the "bacon" and retrieve it for their respective teams. That is traditional Steal the Bacon.

Variations

1. Call two or three numbers at a time.
2. Students can also try to tag the one who steals the "bacon" and take the "bacon" away from him or her.
3. Use a candy bar as the "bacon." The victor can eat the candy bar when he or she makes it back to his or her team.
4. Add on stunts. For example, when a number is called, the two students must do five push ups, touch three students in line and then steal the bacon. Here are other examples:
   - Buy a huge pair of underwear and have them put that on.
   - Have the students twirl a hula hoop for five seconds and then steal the bacon.

Unroll-Reroll Race

SPECIAL FEATURES

NUMBER
10-50 PEOPLE

PREP TIME
NONE

TIME REQUIRED
20-30 MINUTES

INDOOR

ACTIVITY LEVEL

CLEANUP LEVEL

GROSS FACTOR

MATERIALS NEEDED

At least two rolls of toilet paper, or one for *each* team
Masking tape

HOW TO PLAY

Divide group into at least two teams. The teams compete to unroll a roll of toilet paper and then reroll it again. However, to make it more interesting, one team will unroll the toilet paper that the other team will reroll. The teams unroll the rolls at the same time. Tell them that they can go up and down floors, in and out of doors, upstairs, around columns—anywhere that is acceptable to you and within the game area. However, they may not break the roll of paper. If a roll does break, they must come to you and get a piece of masking tape to reattach the paper.

When both of the teams completely unroll their toilet paper (leaving the cardboard roll attached, have them each find the end of the opposing team's roll. At a signal from you, they begin to reroll the paper onto the cardboard roll. Of course, it is easier to unroll than to reroll.

If your group is large or if you choose to do so, you may have more teams competing. However, make sure a different group rolls up the roll from the one who unrolled it.

ADDITIONAL GAMES

When the game is finished, you can play other games with the toilet paper. Let your imagination run wild.
- You can have a "Make a Mummy" contest by having teams see how fast they can wrap one team member in the toilet paper.
- You can tape the rolls into balls with masking tape and play a variation of basketball or volleyball.
- Or you can TP the pastor's house and yard!

Volley Brawl

This game is best played in the sunshine with lots of students on a sand court. However, inside under fluorescent lights in the winter works fine, too.

MATERIALS NEEDED

Volleyball and net
Volleyball court
Bell or whistle
Poster board or newsprint
Felt-tip pen

PREPARATION

Write on poster board or newsprint the following rules for each round:
1. Mixed teams, regular rules.
2. Mixed teams, girls only can make a scoring point. Guys "feed" volleyball to girls. Suspend the three hit rule, but allow no more than five hits before attempt at scoring.
3. Girls only.
4. Guys only.
5. Mixed teams, guys only can score. Girls feed ball to guys. Suspend three hit rule as in 2.
6. Mixed teams with backs to the net. Anyone can score.
7. Volley Brawl round in which the entire team is on the court, anyone can score. Suspend three touch rule.

HOW TO PLAY

Divide the students into two teams with an even mix of guys and girls on each team. The game is divided into seven 3-minute sessions or rounds. After three minutes of play, blow a whistle or ring a bell, then the next round is changed with new players, new rules, etc. Give the groups 30 seconds between rounds to organize for the next round.

Variations

Additional rounds can be invented. Here are more suggestions:
• Stationary round, professional positioning—This means that the

students have to stay planted in the regulation positions of three rows, three to a row. No one is allowed to move her or his feet. They stay planted.

- Stationary round, any position allowable—This means that the students have to stay planted in any place they choose. It can be four in the front, two in the rear, and three in the middle, or any configuration they wish to try. **Note:** In this round you may allow them to move between points.

- Note: For large groups, multiple teams can compete with playoffs between two highest scores. Competition can continue over time (i.e., four weeks).

Volley Brawl is one of those games that often becomes legendary as the years pass.

Water Wars

"Just when you thought it was safe to go back in the water...."

MATERIALS NEEDED

Three red felt-tip pens
Three blue felt-tip pens
Several children's watercolor books
Masking tape
Lots of water balloons

PREPARATION

Buy the children's watercolor books that have the color in the paper and all you need to do is add water to bring out the color. Divide students into two teams—Red and Blue. Each team is given a secret operation base and the same amount of water balloons.

Each team can fill their own supply of water balloons. Each team is then given three felt-tip pens (or similar objects) in the team's color to be hidden by them somewhere on the ministry grounds. The objective is to prevent location and capture of the objects by the other team, but they must be visible.

HOW TO PLAY

Give each team member a page from a child's watercolor book (one of those books that you can buy in discount stores that makes colors when water is applied). One of these watercolor pages is taped to each player's back. The appearance of the colors on this page will indicate that a water balloon hit has occurred. A few drops doesn't count as a hit; there must be a large water spot to count as a hit. When a player is hit, he or she must stop immediately until a new watercolor page can be brought by a team member to be retaped to his or her back.

Offensive players attempt to "capture" the other team's felt-tip pens and take them back to their home base. Defensive players attempt to protect their pens by throwing water balloons at the enemy team members to prevent them from bringing them back to their base. If an enemy carrying the captured pen sustains a water balloon hit, the defenders may recapture their pen and return it to home base before the enemy gets another page.

The game continues until all three of one team's markers are captured and imprisoned in the other base, or until all water balloons/watercolor pages have been used up.

NIGHT TIME - GLOW STICKS

SPECIAL FEATURES

NUMBER
5-35 PEOPLE

PREP TIME
30 MINUTES

TIME REQUIRED
3-5 MINUTES

INDOOR

ACTIVITY LEVEL

CLEANUP LEVEL

GROSS FACTOR

What's Missing?

MATERIALS NEEDED

Sheets of newsprint or poster board
A black felt-tip pen

PREPARATION

Cut sheets of newsprint or poster board into 2-inch by 18- to 24-inch long strips. Write on each strip a phrase from a familiar passage of Scripture, such as the Ten Commandments (see Exodus 20:1-17), the Lord's Prayer (see Matthew 6:9-13), the Beatitudes (see Matthew 5:3-11), the Twenty-Third Psalm, the Gifts of the Spirit (see 1 Corinthians 12:4-10), the Fruit of the Spirit (see Galatians 5:22,23), etc. The phrases need to be complete thoughts so that they are recognizable parts of these familiar passages.

For example, the Lord's Prayer would look something like this:

Our Father in heaven
Hallowed be your name
Your kingdom come
Your will be done
On earth as it is in heaven
Give us today our daily bread
Forgive us our debts
As we also have forgiven our debtors
And lead us not into temptation
But deliver us from the evil one

HOW TO PLAY

The game is quick and simple. Tape all the strips for the passage, except one, on a board or wall. Have students guess what is missing, then they must tell what *is* supposed to be in the missing section. You can give a score for each correct answer, or simply use this game as a transition between activities, such as between game time and Bible study time.

The Lord's Prayer is the easiest one and is best to use as an example or a warm-up. Most of the other suggested passages will be a challenge. You can keep these strips and use them at various times, leaving out a different strip each time.

Variation

Make two copies of a passage and mix them up. Then have two teams race to put them in order.

SPECIAL FEATURES

NUMBER
15-50 PEOPLE

PREP TIME
10 MINUTES

TIME REQUIRED
60-90 MINUTES

IN/OUTDOOR

ACTIVITY LEVEL

CLEANUP LEVEL

GROSS FACTOR

When We Were Young Games

Psychologists tell us we must occasionally "regress in service to the ego," which is a weird way of saying that once in a while it does us good to be a child again.

When We Were Young Games (WWWYG) is a collection of games that your students probably haven't played since adolescence kicked in, unless they baby-sit for a career, help with children's Sunday School classes, or they are a few sandwiches short of a picnic.

MATERIALS NEEDED

Large rubber playground balls
Beanbags
Chalk
Jump ropes
Pieces of cloth for flags, blindfolds, or "hankies"
Cones for marking boundaries, etc.

HOW TO PLAY

WWWY Games feature the original versions of childhood games such as:

Ring Around the Rosy	Drop the Hanky
Duck, Duck, Goose	Steal the Bacon
Kick the Can	Tag
Red Rover	Jump Rope
Hopscotch	Kickball

and any other game they might have played as youngsters. It can be a hilarious time of playing and remembering "when we were young." Be prepared to play a couple of games of your choice, then allow the students to suggest a list of games they remember. Let them choose a game or two from their list.

Tip: Some students will see themselves as "too cool" to participate if you advertise the actual games in WWWYG, so don't mention what they will be doing, or some may skip the meeting. However, once they are there, you'll have little trouble getting them to play.

SPECIAL FEATURES

NUMBER
15-50 PEOPLE

PREP TIME
20 MINUTES

TIME REQUIRED
10 MINUTES

OUTDOOR
OUT

ACTIVITY LEVEL

CLEANUP LEVEL

GROSS FACTOR

REQUIREMENTS

Winter Water Balloons

An outdoor, cold weather water balloon fight works well on a retreat or during a daylong winter activity. Have students dress warmly, covering all body parts with coats, snow pants, etc. Make sure that this is done near the meeting place. It will move quickly and the students will want to get warm again, but it is a pushing-the-limits kind of goofy game that will become legend in the years to come.

MATERIALS NEEDED

Several packages of water balloons

PREPARATION

Have the water balloons filled ahead of time. Store them in two (one for each team) large plastic trash bags or trash cans in a warm place. Don't let the water balloons freeze!

HOW TO PLAY

Divide students into two teams. Give them boundary lines so that they do not get too far from the building. Watch for students who may be getting too cold. Limit the playing time so that students do not get hypothermia.

Use good judgment and do not play this if the temperatures are too cold or the wind chill too low. It can be very safe and fun, but only if you use good judgment.

Have an alternate game planned in case the weather is too cold or too windy.

Serve hot drinks or food after the water balloon fight to help students warm up.

SPECIAL FEATURES

NUMBER

15-100 PEOPLE

PREP TIME

NONE

TIME REQUIRED

15-20 MINUTES

OUTDOOR

ACTIVITY LEVEL

CLEANUP LEVEL

GROSS FACTOR

You're All It

HOW TO PLAY

This game is like regular tag only *everyone* is It. Everyone runs around and tags everyone else. When a person is tagged, he or she leaves the playing area and sits down. The last person standing is the winner!

Apple-Eating Contest

MATERIALS NEEDED

Three cored apples
String

PREPARATION

Prior to the game cut out the center (the core) of the three apples. Tie a three-foot string through the center and tightly around the outside of each of the three apples.

HOW TO PLAY

Ask for six volunteers and divide the six volunteers into three teams of two each. One person on each team will hold (the Holder) the apple while the other person will attempt to eat it (the Eater). Have the Eaters kneel down and the Holder will hold the apple at the level of the Eater's face. At your signal the Eaters will begin eating the apples without using their hands or any part of their bodies except their mouths. The Holders may not allow the apples to touch any part of their bodies. The first one to eat his or her apple wins.

Jello-Dropping Contest

SPECIAL FEATURES

NUMBER
6 VOLUNTEERS

PREP TIME
10 MINUTES

TIME REQUIRED
5 MINUTES

IN/OUTDOOR
IN OUT

ACTIVITY LEVEL

CLEANUP LEVEL

GROSS FACTOR

SPECIAL FEATURES

NUMBER
6-8 VOLUNTEERS

PREP TIME
1 MINUTE

TIME REQUIRED
5 MINUTES

IN/OUTDOOR
IN OUT

ACTIVITY LEVEL

CLEANUP LEVEL

GROSS FACTOR

Baby Feeding

MATERIALS NEEDED

Three or four jars of baby food
Three or four plastic spoons
Several towels
A sheet of plastic

PREPARATION

Spread the plastic sheet on the floor of the playing area.

HOW TO PLAY

Have three or four pairs come forward. One person on each team is to lie down on their backs forming a side-by-side line on the floor. Then have the other team members lie down on their backs so their heads are touching their partners' heads and their feet are pointing in the opposite direction. Put a towel on each player's chest to protect clothing. Give one member on each team a jar of baby food and a plastic spoon. This team member is to feed his or her partner the entire jar of baby food! Because they are on their backs and really can't see each other, this becomes quite a mess! First pair with an empty jar wins!

Balls and Boxes

An all-time favorite—this game works best as one event during a time of several competitions such as a game night, lock-in or retreat.

MATERIALS NEEDED

A makeshift table made out of a piece of plywood placed on two supports, *or* made out of one or two large cardboard boxes

Eight boxes of varying sizes, to cover various sizes of sports balls

Bedsheets to cover the makeshift table

Seven different types of sports balls (i.e., tennis, softball, football, etc.)

An aluminum pie pan

Whipped cream

PREPARATION

This will have to be set up ahead of time and, if at all possible, in an area separate from the rest of the activities. Make a table out of plywood on two supports such as sawhorses (or use a large cardboard box such as a refrigerator box). Cut a head-sized hole in the plywood (or one long side of the cardboard box). Cover the table with bedsheets, cutting a hole to match the hole in the table. Set the eight boxes on the table, and place the seventh box over the hole you have cut through the table. Volunteer one of your popular students (someone who loves to play practical jokes is the perfect candidate) to sit under the table with his or her head sticking up through the hole and covered by the box. Under the rest of the boxes place the various types of sports balls. When the player lifts box number seven, this person is to scream at them. This usually surprises the person and everyone gets a good laugh.

HOW TO PLAY

Ask for four volunteers to come up front. Tell them that they will be timed as they one at a time lift each box and name the type of ball under it. The goal is to go through all of the boxes and name all of the balls faster than the other three. Build this up and tell them that the faster the better! Have three of the volunteers leave the room so they

SPECIAL FEATURES

NUMBER
5 VOLUNTEERS

PREP TIME
60+ MINUTES

TIME REQUIRED
10-20 MINUTES

IN/OUTDOOR

ACTIVITY LEVEL

CLEANUP LEVEL

GROSS FACTOR

cannot see or hear what happens to the first participant. Then have each participant compete.

Now here's the double whammy! Clue in your last participant and let him or her know exactly what is going on. But do not let the student under the box know what is going on. Give this fourth student the whipped cream pie and when he or she lifts that seventh box (and is screamed at by the student under the box) have him or her squish a pie in the popular student's face.

Banana Split-Eating Contest

MATERIALS NEEDED

A half-gallon of ice cream
A container of whipped butter (or margarine)
Four bananas
Four bowls
Various ice cream toppings (chocolate syrup, whipped
    cream, nuts, etc.)
A table and four chairs

PREPARATION

Prepare the banana splits beforehand and keep refrigerated. Prepare three normal banana splits. Prepare the fourth one using whipped butter instead of ice cream. Disguise all four with lots of whipped cream and numerous toppings. Set up the table with all four chairs on one side of the table, facing the audience.

HOW TO PLAY

Ask for four volunteers to come forward and have them sit on the chairs facing the group. Bring out the four banana splits and hand one to each person. Tell them the objective is to eat the banana splits as quickly as they can, without a spoon. The first one done wins. On the word "go," have them start. It takes a few minutes for the butter-eating person to figure out there is something wrong because the nuts, chocolate and whipped cream disguise the butter at first.

SPECIAL FEATURES

NUMBER
4 VOLUNTEERS

PREP TIME
30 MINUTES

TIME REQUIRED
5 MINUTES

IN/OUTDOOR
IN OUT

ACTIVITY LEVEL

CLEANUP LEVEL

GROSS FACTOR

SPECIAL FEATURES

NUMBER
3 VOLUNTEERS

PREP TIME
5 MINUTES

TIME REQUIRED
5 MINUTES

IN/OUTDOOR
IN OUT

ACTIVITY LEVEL

CLEANUP LEVEL

GROSS FACTOR

Banana-Eating Contest

MATERIALS NEEDED

Three large bowls
Six to nine bananas
Three blindfolds
A table and three chairs
A sheet of plastic

PREPARATION

Set up the table and chairs with the chairs facing the audience. Cover the table with the plastic sheet. Set the bowls on the table with two to three bananas in each bowl.

HOW TO PLAY

This game is hilarious if done right. Be sure to carefully choose your "volunteers"—they need to be good sports. After you have chosen three students to come up front, tell them they are going to compete against one another in a banana-eating contest. The only trick is that they will be blindfolded. After they are blindfolded, have them sit down on the chairs and on the count of one-two-three-go they begin peeling and eating the bananas in front of them. After they get started, secretly take the blindfolds off of two of the players and watch the third person continue the contest all alone! If the right student is chosen, this is very funny. But be careful because it could backfire!

Candle Shoot-Out

MATERIALS NEEDED

Three candles
Three candleholders
Three squirt guns
Matches
A table

PREPARATION

Set the table up in front of the room. Fill the squirt guns with water. Put the three candles in the candleholders and set them on the table.

HOW TO PLAY

Ask for six volunteers and pair them up. Have one person from each pair kneel behind the table with a candle set about 18 inches in front of their faces. The persons from each will then kneel on the opposite side of the table, facing their "other halves" about five feet away from them. Light the candles and give the second person in each pair a squirt gun filled with water. On the word "go," the "shooters" are to try and squirt out the lighted candle in front of their partners. Watch that the "victims" do not blow out the candle. The first light out, wins!

SPECIAL FEATURES

NUMBER
6 VOLUNTEERS

PREP TIME
5 MINUTES

TIME REQUIRED
10 MINUTES

IN/OUTDOOR
IN OUT

ACTIVITY LEVEL

CLEANUP LEVEL

GROSS FACTOR

SPECIAL
FEATURES

NUMBER

4 VOLUNTEERS

PREP TIME

30-60 MINUTES

TIME REQUIRED

5 MINUTES

IN/OUTDOOR

IN OUT

ACTIVITY LEVEL

CLEANUP LEVEL

GROSS FACTOR

REQUIREMENTS

S

Caramel Apple-Eating Contest

MATERIALS NEEDED

Three apples
One onion
A bag or two of caramel candies
Four popsicle sticks
Four paper plates
A rectangular cake pan or cookie sheet
A table and four chairs

PREPARATION

Several hours before the meeting, prepare the caramel "apples." Push a stick into each of the apples and the onion. Melt the caramels according to the package directions. Dip the apples and the onion into the melted caramels, place them in a pan or on a cookie sheet and place into the refrigerator to cool.

Set up the table and chairs facing the group. Place each of the "apples" on a separate paper plate and set them on the table, one in front of each chair.

HOW TO PLAY

Ask for four volunteers for a caramel apple-eating contest. Have them each sit in a chair. Tell them they must race to see who can eat their apples the fastest. Tell them to begin when you say, "Go!" It takes a few seconds, but eventually the onion-eating person figures it out.

Cartoon Creation

MATERIALS NEEDED

The comics pages of a newspaper
Pens or pencils
Overhead projector and transparency

PREPARATION

Cut out a simple cartoon from your local newspaper. Enlarge it and remove the captions or speech from the balloons. Make three copies on plain paper and one copy on an overhead transparency.

HOW TO PLAY

Ask for three volunteers and give each of them a paper copy of the cartoon. Give them three minutes to fill in the blanks. Tell them the funniest one will win. After they have completed their papers, bring them back up front and put the transparency up so all can see. Then read the three captions written by the three volunteers. The funniest one wins! You can have the rest of the group vote.

Variation

Divide the group into teams and have them work together on the captions.

SPECIAL FEATURES

NUMBER
3 VOLUNTEERS

PREP TIME
15-20 MINUTES

TIME REQUIRED
15 MINUTES

IN/OUTDOOR
IN OUT

ACTIVITY LEVEL

CLEANUP LEVEL

GROSS FACTOR

SPECIAL FEATURES

NUMBER
6 VOLUNTEERS

PREP TIME
10 MINUTES

TIME REQUIRED
5-15 MINUTES

IN/OUTDOOR
IN OUT

ACTIVITY LEVEL

CLEANUP LEVEL

GROSS FACTOR

Donut Dunkin'

MATERIALS NEEDED

Three donuts
Three towels or one large plastic sheet
String
Chocolate syrup
Three bowls

PREPARATION

Tie a three-foot length of string through the hole and around the side on each of the donuts.

HOW TO PLAY

Ask for six volunteers and then pair them up. Have the one person in each pair lie down on a towel or plastic sheet. Give the second person in each pair a donut with the string tied around it. Each standing partner holds the end of the string and dips the donut into a bowl of chocolate placed next to his or her partner's head. The object is for the ones lying down, without using their hands, to eat all of the donut. Their partners must dunk the donuts into the chocolate after each bite. First one done wins!

Egg Roulette

MATERIALS NEEDED

Twelve eggs
A pan
Optional: Easter egg dye

PREPARATION

The day (or several hours) before, boil eleven of the eggs, leaving one uncooked. Discard any eggs that may have cracked while boiling. If you want to add some color to the activity, dye all of the eggs, including the raw egg. When the eggs are dry, return them to the carton and refrigerate until you need them.

HOW TO PLAY

Ask for eight volunteers and have them come forward. Line them up side-by-side and tell them that they are about to play a game of egg roulette. Each of them is to pick an egg from the carton and crack it over the head of the person next to them. This continues until the raw egg is broken.

SPECIAL FEATURES

NUMBER
8 VOLUNTEERS

PREP TIME
15-30 MINUTES

TIME REQUIRED
5 MINUTES

IN/OUTDOOR

ACTIVITY LEVEL

CLEANUP LEVEL

GROSS FACTOR

SPECIAL FEATURES

NUMBER
8 VOLUNTEERS

PREP TIME
5 MINUTES

TIME REQUIRED
5 MINUTES

OUTDOOR
OUT

ACTIVITY LEVEL

CLEANUP LEVEL

GROSS FACTOR

Eggs and Stockings Chicken Fight

MATERIALS NEEDED

Four knee-high stockings
Four eggs
Newspapers (or cardboard rolls from paper towels, plastic
  wrap or gift wrap)

HOW TO PLAY

Ask for four guys to volunteer and assign each of them a female partner. Place a knee-high stocking over each guy's head and put a raw
egg in the toe of the stocking so that the egg rests on top of their
heads. Next, the girls get up on their partners' shoulders for a chicken
fight. Give each girl a section of rolled-up newspaper (or a cardboard
roll). On the signal from you, the girls are to try and protect their guys
while trying to break the other guys' eggs. The last egg remaining
unbroken wins!

Eggs-in-a-Bottle

MATERIALS NEEDED

Two dozen eggs
Three clean, empty soft drink bottles
A table and three chairs
A sheet of plastic
Sponges
Towels

PREPARATION

Set up the table in front of the room with the three chairs behind it facing the audience. Cover the table with a sheet of plastic. Place the three bottles on the table.

HOW TO PLAY

Ask for three volunteers to come forward and sit down at the table facing the rest of the group. Instruct them that on the word "go," they will begin to break the first egg, then squeeze as much of the egg into the bottle as possible. The first person to fill up the bottle wins!

Tip: Have sponges and towels ready for clean-up. Also, have adult leaders prepared to thwart any ideas of an egg fight following the contest.

SPECIAL FEATURES

NUMBER
3 VOLUNTEERS

PREP TIME
5-10 MINUTES

TIME REQUIRED
5 MINUTES

IN/OUTDOOR
IN OUT

ACTIVITY LEVEL

CLEANUP LEVEL

GROSS FACTOR

Guys, Gloves and Pantyhose

SPECIAL FEATURES

NUMBER

3 VOLUNTEERS

PREP TIME

1 MINUTE

TIME REQUIRED

5-10 MINUTES

IN/OUTDOOR

IN OUT

ACTIVITY LEVEL

CLEANUP LEVEL

GROSS FACTOR

MATERIALS NEEDED

Three blindfolds
Three pairs of large gloves
Three pairs of pantyhose
Three chairs

HOW TO PLAY

Ask for three or four guys, preferably guys who think they are pretty macho. Have them sit on chairs facing the crowd. They are to remove their shoes.

Tell them that they are to reach forward and pick up the pantyhose that will be laid out on the floor in front of them. They are to pull the pantyhose on over both legs all the way up to their waists. The first one to do this wins. The trick is that they are going to be blindfolded and they will be wearing gloves. When they are blindfolded and "begloved" say, "Go." Have a camera ready!

Impromptu Games

Ice Fishing

Materials Needed

Two to three dozen marbles
One large tub of water, large enough for at least three large
  feet at a time
A large bag of ice
Three large towels
Three chairs
A sheet of plastic

Preparation

About 30 to 40 minutes before doing this activity, put about two to three dozen marbles in the tub, then fill the tub about half full with ice and water. This will give the ice time to melt and make the water especially frigid. Lay the plastic sheet on the floor and set the tub of water in the middle of it with the chairs arranged in a half circle around the tub.

How to Play

Ask for three volunteers. Have them sit in the chairs facing the group, then take off their shoes and socks. Tell them they are going fishing. Their task is to use the toes of one foot to try and pull out as many marbles as they can in one minute. The one who pulls out the most marbles wins. The only trick is that the container of water is also full of ice water.

Option: You can exchange the marbles for olives, pickles, etc.

SPECIAL FEATURES

NUMBER
3 VOLUNTEERS

PREP TIME
10 MINUTES

TIME REQUIRED
5 MINUTES

IN/OUTDOOR
IN OUT

ACTIVITY LEVEL

CLEANUP LEVEL

GROSS FACTOR

SPECIAL FEATURES

NUMBER
3-4 VOLUNTEERS

PREP TIME
5 MINUTES

TIME REQUIRED
10 MINUTES

IN/OUTDOOR
IN OUT

ACTIVITY LEVEL

CLEANUP LEVEL

GROSS FACTOR

Ketchup Race

This crazy game is fun to watch because it creates such a huge mess, so plan on playing this game outside or cover the playing area with plenty of plastic!

MATERIALS NEEDED

Nine to 12 fresh, ripe tomatoes
Three to four clean, empty soft drink bottles
Optional: A sheet of plastic (if playing this inside)

PREPARATION

If you are not doing this outside, lay down a sheet of plastic on the floor and set the soft drink bottles on the plastic.

HOW TO PLAY

Ask three or four volunteers to come forward. Have the volunteers kneel down in front of a soft drink bottle facing the crowd. Give them each three tomatoes and tell them that on the word "Go," they have one minute to make as much ketchup as they can. Whoever squeezes the most tomatoes into the soft drink bottle wins.

The Know-My-Kid Game

This game can be a powerful tool for bringing families closer together in a fun and humorous fashion. Try it! Adapt it!

PREPARATION

During a session a week or two before an upcoming parents' meeting, give the students the survey on the following pages or make up a survey of your own. Choose three surveys with the most humorous or interesting answers. These will be the contestants for "The Know-My-Kid Game" that will be played during the parents' meeting. Make sure that the students you choose don't mind and that their parents will attend. (Both the students and their parents need to be good sports.)

HOW TO PLAY

At the parents' meeting, invite the parents of your chosen contestants up front. Read the questions and ask the parents for the response that they think their teenager picked. Parents receive points when they guess correctly. If you use the questions on the prepared survey, don't use every question. Select about six or eight of the best questions.

This game can be used as a lead-in for more serious discussions of communication and family harmony. For debriefing after the game, you can ask parents what they thought of the game, what one thing they would like to tell their sons or daughters about how they feel towards them, and how students and parents can build each other up as a family united in Christ.

Appropriate Scriptures to use include Romans 14:13,19; 1 Corinthians 13:1-8; Ephesians 4:25-27; 6:1-4; Colossians 2:2,3; 3:20,21; 1 Thessalonians 5:11; James 3:2-12; 4:1-3.

Variation

Do this in reverse. Ask parents to fill out similar surveys and have students decide how their parents answered.

SPECIAL FEATURES

NUMBER
3+ VOLUNTEERS

PREP TIME
30 MINUTES

TIME REQUIRED
30 MINUTES

INDOOR

ACTIVITY LEVEL

CLEANUP LEVEL

GROSS FACTOR

The Do-You-Know-Me Survey

Please complete as much of this survey as you feel comfortable doing. **Note:** Some of these answers might be shared in front of the youth group and parents. Be open and sensitive, yet honest!

1. My parents are as excited about going to church as if...
   A. Church was giving away free money.
   B. Church was as routine as going to work.
   C. Church was like getting a root canal.

2. In a discussion about "the birds and the bees"...
   A. My dad told me the facts of life.
   B. My mom told me the facts of life.
   C. I had to tell my mom and dad the facts of life.

3. My parents treat me as if...
   A. I'm the most important thing in their lives.
   B. I'm somewhere between irritating and annoying.
   C. Slavery is still legal and they're my masters.

4. An appropriate T-shirt for my parents would read...
   A. "Parent of the World's Greatest Kid"
   B. "Take My Kid—Please"
   C. "Property of the Insane Asylum"

5. My grades at school make my parents...
   A. Proud as can be.
   B. Loud and upset.
   C. Claim they don't know me.

6. Which type of breakfast cereal best describes your parents...
   A. Corn Flakes
   B. Grape Nuts
   C. Fruity Pebbles

7. My communication with my parents is...
   A. Great—we talk all the time.
   B. Okay—they hear from me at least once a day.
   C. Not so good—our last meaningful talk was when I was seven years old.

8. In your family, who is the loudest snorer?

9. What is your mom's favorite TV show?

10. What is the meanest trick a parent has ever played on you?

11. What holiday is the biggest deal in your family?

12. What would your parents do if they won a million dollars?

13. Who is the best cook in your family?

14. What is the worst chore you have to do?

15. What is the neatest way a parent shows you that you are loved?

16. When is your curfew?

17. What do you want to be?

18. What is the most common way for your parents to embarrass you in front of your friends?

19. If you could tell your parents just one thing about how you feel about them, what would it be?

20. If my parents could tell me just one thing about how they feel about me, I think it would be...

Impromptu
Games

Lemonade-Eating Contest

MATERIALS NEEDED

A box of individual sugar packets
A lemon for each participant
Large glasses of water

PREPARATION

Cut each lemon into quarters. Fill the glasses with cold water.

HOW TO PLAY

Ask for three volunteers to come forward and have them seated in chairs facing the rest of the group. Give each volunteer two packs of sugar, a lemon (cut into quarters) and a large glass of cold water. On the word "go," they must first eat the sugar, then eat the lemon and finally drink the water. The first one to finish the sugar, lemon and glass of water is the winner. The results are hilarious! Be sure to have a camera ready!

Lipstick Contest

MATERIALS NEEDED

Three tubes of lipstick, bright red is the best

HOW TO PLAY

Ask for six volunteers—three guys and three girls. Pair up each guy and with a girl. Each girl will hold the metal tube part of lipstick in her mouth with the red tip facing outward. Each guy will then proceed to apply the lipstick to his mouth by moving only his mouth (with his hands held behind his back). Give the pairs one minute to apply the lipstick. You can have judges determine who put the lipstick on the best, or have the whole group vote.

SPECIAL FEATURES

NUMBER
6 VOLUNTEERS

PREP TIME
NONE

TIME REQUIRED
5 MINUTES

IN/OUTDOOR
IN OUT

ACTIVITY LEVEL

CLEANUP LEVEL

GROSS FACTOR

SPECIAL
FEATURES

NUMBER

6 VOLUNTEERS

PREP TIME

1 MINUTE

TIME REQUIRED

5-10 MINUTES

IN/OUTDOOR

IN OUT

ACTIVITY LEVEL

CLEANUP LEVEL

GROSS FACTOR

Oogie Boogie

MATERIALS NEEDED

Three large sponges
A container of water
Three chairs

HOW TO PLAY

Tell the group that you are going to see who is the strongest guy in the group. Have three strong guys come forward. Then choose three gals of about equal size (to one another) to come forward as well. Have the girls sit in chairs facing the crowd. Have each guy stand behind a girl also facing the crowd. On the count of three, the guys are to lift the girls by their elbows and hold them up for as long as they can. When the girls are in the air, have a leader sneak a soaking wet sponge onto each of the chairs. After a moment, have the guys give in and set the girls back down. It takes a second before they realize that their seats are soaking wet!

Pass the Pie

MATERIALS NEEDED

One or more aluminum pie pans
One to two aerosol cans of whipped cream
A sheet of plastic
CD or tape and player

PREPARATION

Fill one or more aluminum pie pans with whipped cream. Although you use only one pie at a time, it is a good idea to have more than one ready to save time refilling the pan.

HOW TO PLAY

Ask for eight volunteers and have them line up side-by-side across the front of the group. Give the first person in line the pie pan filled with whipped cream. As music is played they are to pass the pie from one person to the next. The person playing the music should be blind-folded or have his or view of the volunteers blocked so that he or she can be completely impartial. When the music stops the person left holding the pie has the option of hitting the person on the left or right in the face with the pie. Then the one who is hit with the pie sits down. The music starts again and the pie is passed until the music stops again. Play continues until the person left holding the pie gets to hit the only other person still standing, then the game is over. When the pie reaches the end of the line of eight people, have the last person pass it back the other way.

    Tip: Any person holding a pie can only hold the pie for up to two seconds, and no longer.

SPECIAL FEATURES

NUMBER
2 VOLUNTEERS

PREP TIME
5 MINUTES

TIME REQUIRED
5 MINUTES

INDOOR

ACTIVITY LEVEL

CLEANUP LEVEL

GROSS FACTOR

Ping-Pong Bounce

This game can put a guy against a girl, or one member of one team against a member of another team, or one grade level against another, etc.

MATERIALS NEEDED

Two or more ping-pong balls (depending on the number of competitors)
Two or more ping-pong paddles (depending on the number of competitors)

HOW TO PLAY

Select two or more volunteers or have a representative from each team come forward. The object of the competition is to take a ping-pong paddle and bounce a ping-pong ball up and down as many times as possible without missing the ball. The trick is that the person must hit the ball on one side of the paddle and then alternate to the other side. This can be done with both competitors bouncing their balls at the same time, or with each one doing it separately. This continues back and forth until the ball is missed. Have the whole group count the number of hits for each person out loud. The person with the most hits wins!

Santa Beards

This is a great Christmas game.

MATERIALS NEEDED

Three cans of shaving cream
Three towels
Three chairs

HOW TO PLAY

Have three guys volunteer to come forward and then ask for three gals to volunteer. Have the guys sit in the chairs. Wrap towels around their necks and chests.

Give each girl a can of shaving cream. Tell the girls they are to create the best looking Santa beard on their partners. This is not a timed contest so tell them to take their time and try to create the very best beard they can. Give them about three to four minutes to complete the beards. Have the rest of the group vote for the best beard.

SPECIAL FEATURES

NUMBER
6 VOLUNTEERS

PREP TIME
NONE

TIME REQUIRED
10 MINUTES

IN/OUTDOOR
IN OUT

ACTIVITY LEVEL

CLEANUP LEVEL

GROSS FACTOR

SPECIAL FEATURES

NUMBER
2+ VOLUNTEERS

PREP TIME
NONE

TIME REQUIRED
5 MINUTES

IN/OUTDOOR
IN OUT

ACTIVITY LEVEL

CLEANUP LEVEL

GROSS FACTOR

Space Helmet

MATERIALS NEEDED

Several pairs of new surgical gloves

HOW TO PLAY

Ask for as many volunteers as there are gloves. Give each person a surgical glove. Have each of them place their gloves over their heads and their noses (but not their mouths!). At your signal tell them they are to blow up the glove by blowing through their noses. The first one to blow up and pop their glove wins! The results are hilarious. Have your camera ready for this one!

Stick 'Em Up

MATERIALS NEEDED

A large jar of peanut butter
Three rubber spatulas
A large container of Planters Cheez Balls
Three plastic bags

PREPARATION

Divide the Planters Cheez Balls between the three plastic bags.

HOW TO PLAY

Ask for six volunteers. Pair them up. Have three of the volunteers stand facing the group. Have the partners for each put smooth peanut butter all over their faces, using the rubber spatulas. Then have each of the partners stand about five feet away from them. Give each of the partners (without the peanut butter on their faces) a bag of Cheez Balls. On the word "go," have them toss the Cheez Balls at their partners' faces trying to get the balls to stick. After one minute, the team with the most Cheez Balls stuck wins!

Sticky Dime

MATERIALS NEEDED

A dime
A chair

HOW TO PLAY

Ask for three volunteers and have them come forward. Have two of them leave the room. Tell the remaining person that you are going to stick a dime on his or her forehead and he or she is to contort his or her face until the dime falls off his or her forehead. Demonstrate this by pressing a dime firmly on his or her forehead. Time the participant, telling him or her this is just a practice round (this usually takes a few seconds). Praise the participant for his or her success and say that now, for the real contest, he or she will be timed.

This time, instead of actually pressing the dime on his or her forehead, hide the dime and press only with your finger (it will feel the same to the person). Press hard for three or four seconds and then remove your finger and say "Go." Have the crowd encourage the student to do his or her best to get that dime off. Continue this until he or she finally realizes that there is in fact nothing on his or her forehead.

After the first person is let in on the trick, bring in the other participants one at a time and repeat the process.

Team Skiing

MATERIALS NEEDED

Six four-foot-long 2x4s
Duct tape

HOW TO PLAY

Ask for six volunteers: three guys and three gals. Pair the guys and gals and tell them they are going to have a "ski" race against the other teams. Give each couple two of the 2x4s. Have several students help each participant tape their feet securely onto the 2x4s—both left legs on one board and both right legs on the other with one person behind the other. When done, each pair has all four feet taped onto their "skis." Have the helpers help the couples stand up. They cannot move unless they move together. On the signal "Go," they are to "ski" together around a designated course and then return to the starting point. The first pair to return wins.

SPECIAL
FEATURES

NUMBER
4 VOLUNTEERS

PREP TIME
1 MINUTE

TIME REQUIRED
5 MINUTES

IN/OUTDOOR
IN OUT

ACTIVITY LEVEL

CLEANUP LEVEL

GROSS FACTOR

Tootsie Dogs

MATERIALS NEEDED

Four large Tootsie Rolls
Four paper plates

HOW TO PLAY

Ask for four volunteers to come forward. Give each one a large Tootsie Roll and ask them to begin chewing. Give them each a paper plate and tell them they have one minute to form a "Tootsie dog" in their mouths with the Tootsie Roll they are chewing. After one minute they are to spit the Tootsie dog onto their plates. Have adult leaders judge. The best Tootsie dog wins!

Upside-Down Soda Contest

SPECIAL FEATURES

NUMBER
3 VOLUNTEERS

PREP TIME
5 MINUTES

TIME REQUIRED
5 MINUTES

IN/OUTDOOR
IN OUT

ACTIVITY LEVEL

CLEANUP LEVEL

GROSS FACTOR

MATERIALS NEEDED

Three cans of soda pop
A large sheet of plastic

PREPARATION

Lay the sheet of plastic on the floor where the contest will take place.

HOW TO PLAY

Ask for three volunteers and have them stand in front of the group. Place a can of soda on the floor in front of them and tell them they are going to have a soda-guzzling contest. No big deal, except that they must stand on their heads to do it. Have someone help them get on their heads and then hold their feet. Once they are in place say "Go" and watch the chaos! First one done wins.

* UP SIDE DOWN NIGHT

What Would You Do for a Dollar?

This is a crazy, ongoing game that can last for weeks.

MATERIALS NEEDED

A small plastic bowl and/or glass
Any combination of foods or liquids to mix
Several one dollar bills

HOW TO PLAY

To begin with, ask students what they would do for a dollar. Ask "Would you eat/drink this?" Then concoct a nasty mixture of foods or liquids in the bowl or glass in front of the whole group, but don't get too carried away the first week.

For example, make the concoction a mixture of mayonnaise, Tabasco sauce, lemon juice, soft drink and grape jelly. Ask for a volunteer, assuring them that if they eat/drink this they will get a dollar.

Do the same thing the following week. Then each week make it a little more crazy, a little nastier.

Tip: Have a garbage can nearby just in case.

Whistle and Burp

MATERIALS NEEDED

Crackers
Cans or paper cups of soda pop

PREPARATION

This contest consists of three teams of two members each competing against each other. It's often best when the teams are made up of one guy and one gal.

HOW TO PLAY

The objective is for one member from each team to eat two crackers and then, upon completion, whistle. After that team member has whistled (and the judge has heard it!), the next team member guzzles a soft drink as quickly as possible, then burps. The first team to achieve a burp wins.

Variations

You can add to this game by adding team members and stunts that must be performed. For example, a third member would have to drink a glass of water then cough, a fourth would eat a teaspoon of peanut butter then whistle, a fifth would chew a piece of gum then blow a bubble, etc.

SPECIAL FEATURES

NUMBER
6 VOLUNTEERS

PREP TIME
1 MINUTE

TIME REQUIRED
5 MINUTES

IN/OUTDOOR
IN   OUT

ACTIVITY LEVEL

CLEANUP LEVEL

GROSS FACTOR

Crowdbreakers

crowd \ˈkraud, ˈkrud\ *n* **1** : a large number of people esp. when collected together : THRONG **2 a** : the great body of the people : POPULACE **b** : most of one's peers ‹follow the ~› (from *Merriam Webster's Collegiate Dictionary, Tenth Edition*)

¹breaker \ˈbrā-kər\ *n* **1 a** : one that breaks **b** : a machine or plant for breaking rocks or coal (from *Merriam Webster's Collegiate Dictionary, Tenth Edition*)

Crowdbreakers are activities designed to bring a group together by reducing the "space" between group members. "Space" may mean physical distance between people, but more often it means emotional distance. The purpose of crowdbreakers is to bridge the gaps between individuals so they can get to know one another in a lively and entertaining way. These crowdbreakers can be adjusted to any size group, and usually do not require a lot of prep time except in a few instances that we have marked by icons.

Crowdbreakers, also known as icebreakers, can be brief activities used at the beginning of a session to warm up the group, or they can be longer activities, taking the entire meeting time to complete. The universal intention is to unify the group in fellowship.

—Mark Simone and Joel Lusz

SPECIAL
FEATURES

NUMBER

PREP TIME

NONE

TIME REQUIRED

5-10 MINUTES

American Hero

It's a mystery how this fun icebreaker got its name, but it works!

HOW TO PLAY

First, have all of the guys get in the middle of the room or playing area and tell them to lock arms and legs as tight as they can. The girls will then try to pull guys apart until there is only one guy left. This wild free-for-all is a blast. Not only that, but it does just what it is supposed to do—mixes all the students together.

Now switch and have the girls lock arms and legs, then the guys try to break them apart.

As a reminder to youth leaders: please exercise due caution when using games, crowdbreakers and community builders that are high activity or involve food. Gospel Light cannot be held responsible for any injuries incurred.

The Anthology of Holey Tales

SPECIAL FEATURES

NUMBER

PREP TIME

NONE

TIME REQUIRED

1-5 MINUTES

Students love to tell "tall tales"—stories that obviously did not happen, could never have happened, and likely will never happen. This crowdbreaker gives your group an opportunity to be creative and entertain one another with their stories.

MATERIALS NEEDED

Lifesaver candies

PREPARATION

The week before this activity, ask students to wear their holey socks to the next youth group meeting. Tell them that everyone who does will be awarded a prize.

HOW TO PLAY

As the group gathers for the meeting, ask the students to remove their shoes and leave them at the door. Divide them into groups of three or four, then have everyone show off their best sock holes in their small groups. Give a Lifesaver candy to each person who has a "hole-in-one" sock.

Next, tell the group that you have heard that some of these holes have had amazing origins and that you know for a fact that the current wearers either know the story of the hole, or they have experienced the hole-making event themselves. Tell the small groups to share with one another the how, who, why, when, what and where of the tale of the creation of each of their sock holes. Prompt the students that you are looking for wild, yet nearly believable stories. Have each group select the best story for reporting to the whole group. Or record them on tape (audio or video) and/or write them down for *The Anthology of Holey Tales*.

Another alternative is to have the small groups mix and mingle bits of each member's story for a group story to be told to the whole group.

When this activity is completed, wave your hand in front of your nose and beg the students to put their shoes back on.

SPECIAL FEATURES

NUMBER

PREP TIME

10-15 MINUTES

TIME REQUIRED

10-15 MINUTES

Bags of Fun

This simple icebreaker gets every student mingling and meeting others.

MATERIALS NEEDED

Four small slips of paper
A pen or pencil
Four paper bags, lunch-sized is fine
Four surprises to be put in the bags, your choice

PREPARATION

Write the numbers one, two, three or four on four individual slips of paper—one number on each paper. Plant within the group four students who you have informed ahead of time. These four students each have a slip of numbered paper in his or her pocket.

Prepare four "Bags of Fun"—lunch-size bags with a prize in each bag. Staple the bags closed so no one can peek. These prizes might be a candy bar, a gift certificate, plastic toy or an onion. Let your imagination run wild!

HOW TO PLAY

Have everyone stand up and begin to walk around and mingle, bumping into and meeting other students. At a designated signal—music stops, a whistle blows, or whatever you devise—have the planted person with the number one grab a nearby student and find out that person's name and yell "John has won the first prize." John then picks one of the four "Bags of Fun" held by an adult leader. Whatever is in that bag, John gets. Who knows?!

After the first person picks a prize, have the group continue mingling until all four bags are claimed.

Bogus Introductions

SPECIAL FEATURES

NUMBER

PREP TIME

NONE

TIME REQUIRED

15-20 MINUTES

MATERIALS NEEDED

Paper
Pens or pencils

HOW TO PLAY

This is a hilarious way to introduce a group when there are many new faces. Divide the students into groups of two. No one is to be paired with a person he or she knows well. It's best if they are complete strangers.

Each player needs a pencil and a piece of paper. Give the teams a few minutes to say "Hi" and tell a bit about themselves, then give the following instructions:

> You have now gotten to know your partner better. What I want you to do now is to write an introduction for your partner—a completely bogus introduction. For example: "This is John Smith. John is currently skipping his junior and senior year at high school to lead the surgical unit at Community Hospital where he will be the surgery trainer of new resident doctors. He is not married, believing that commitment to one woman would put all of womankind into a deep depression. So, he dates a different woman every free evening. He loves to field scuba dive, especially in cornfields throughout the Midwest. His dream is to establish lisping as an acceptable language form, and his favorite food is found in the pet section of the local grocery—Kibbles and Bits."

The level of laughter is only exceeded by the amazing creativity the students will display. Promote good introductions and tell the students not to be vicious or offensive. Have them use the paper to jot down a few notes about how they will introduce their partners. After sharing, if you have time, have students stand up and share who they really are.

Comb!
Clean! Count!

This is a really strange competition that will truly break up a crowd.

MATERIALS NEEDED

Lots of cheap plastic combs
Sheets of newsprint
Tables or areas of open floor space

HOW TO PLAY

Divide the students into groups of no more than four per group. Each student is given a comb (or uses his or her own clean comb). Tell students to comb through their hair ten strokes. Then empty the comb and count the number of hairs. The team that produces the most hairs within the forty total strokes wins the competition.

Give the commands, "Comb! Clean! Count!"

This is a great lead-in to a study on Samson, the woman in Luke 7:36-50 who cleaned Jesus' feet with her own hair, or other verses with references to hair. Or just do it to have fun.

Do As I Do

SPECIAL FEATURES

NUMBER

PREP TIME

1-5 MINUTES

TIME REQUIRED

5-10 MINUTES

MATERIALS NEEDED

Small paper cups
Pitchers of water

PREPARATION

The paper cups need to be filled with a little water (about one-quarter of a cup). There are a number of ways you can do this. The first way is to have the cups filled beforehand, placed on trays and ready to pass around just before the activity. Another way would be to fill the cups beforehand, place them on a table near the entrance and have students pick up a paper cup with water as they enter the room. Or yet another would be to give each student a paper cup, then pass around pitchers of water.

HOW TO PLAY

Have the group assemble in the meeting room and give everyone a small paper cup with a little water in each. Tell them you are going to do a toast to commemorate something. Tell them that whoever does this toast exactly like you will win a special prize.

Tell them to repeat everything you do.

Take your cup of water and hold it up in the air and say, "A toast."

They'll repeat.

Continue: "To everyone here," (move your cup to your left).

Let them repeat.

Then say, "And to everyone at home" (move your cup to the right.)

They repeat.

"And to the future." (move your cup straight ahead again).

They repeat.

Then say "Bottoms up!" and pour the water into your mouth, but rather than swallowing it, you'll actually keep the water in your mouth. Bring your hand with the cup in it down as if you've finished the toast and "swallowed" the water. Wait for the audience to do the same. When they are done, spit your water back into your cup (as if

that were the real ending to the toast). Everyone will have already swallowed their water and it will be too late to do anything about it. No prize winners!

Duck, Pig, Cow

SPECIAL FEATURES

NUMBER

30+ PEOPLE

PREP TIME

NONE

TIME REQUIRED

10-15 MINUTES

This works best for large groups of 30 or more.

HOW TO PLAY

Assign one-third of your students to be ducks, another one-third to be pigs and the other one-third to be cows.

Tell them the object of this game is to make their animal sounds as loud as they can and find the other animals. The trick is that they will do this in the dark. Turn out all the lights and tell them to walk around making their sounds and locating the other group members making the same sound. When they find someone making the same sound, they form a group. That group stays together and continues to find more of the same.

After several minutes, tell them you will turn on the light and they are to sit down with their group. The largest group wins. Be sure to do this in total darkness, or a strobe light also works!

Variations

- Use different animals and their sounds.
- Make up new and unusual sounds.
- Assign them things like foods or candy names or colors, and have them yell out their food/candy/color until they find their groups.

SPECIAL FEATURES

NUMBER

PREP TIME

10-15 MINUTES

TIME REQUIRED

15-20 MINUTES

Find and Sign

This activity can begin before your meeting starts as students are coming in and hanging out.

MATERIALS NEEDED

Photocopies of "Find and Sign" sheet, enough for everyone in the group
Pens or pencils

PREPARATION

Design a "Find and Sign" information sheet (see page 135) that applies to your group. Make enough photocopies so that every group member has one.

HOW TO PLAY

As students arrive, give each of them a "Find and Sign" information sheet. Instruct them to get as many signatures from other students as they can. The person with the most signatures wins. Remind them to only sign another's paper if they have honestly done the activity.

When your meeting time starts, collect all of the papers and have an adult leader determine the winner.

Sample Information Sheet

Find and Sign

YOUR NAME:_____

Find at least one person for each of the following categories and have each one sign beside the phrase that describes him or her.

FIND SOMEONE WHO...

Has been to Europe

Is a junior in high school

Was born in Florida

Is wearing purple

Has a Beatles album

Dated Susie

Ate a hamburger last night

Won a beauty pageant

Can whistle

Hates chocolate

Flour Power

MATERIALS NEEDED

10-pound bag of flour
A wooden board or sturdy cardboard
A large bowl
A small piece of wrapped candy
Table knife
A table

PREPARATION

First, set up the table in front of the group. Take a large bowl and pack it up to the top very tightly with the flour. Place the board or sturdy cardboard on top of the bowl. While holding both together firmly, flip the bowl over and place the board on the table. Gently lift the bowl, leaving the flour on the table. If you packed it tightly enough, the flour should retain the shape of the bowl.

HOW TO PLAY

Gently place a small piece of candy on top of the flour.

Now, line up everyone in single file. Give the first person in line a table knife and have him or her carve out a small part of the bowl-shaped pile of flour away from the candy. After each successful carving, have each person give the knife to the next person in line. This continues until the candy finally falls into the remaining flour, then the person who made it fall must pick it out with his or her lips. The result is hilarious!

Gorilla, Gun, Karate

This is a variation of the game "Rock, Paper, Scissors."

MATERIALS NEEDED

Chalk or white board, or overhead projector and transparency
An appropriate writing instrument

PREPARATION

Write the following words on the board or an overhead transparency:

Gorilla kills gun
Gun kills karate
Karate kills gorilla

HOW TO PLAY

Have each group member find a partner. They are to stand back-to-back with their partner and wait for a signal from the leader. When the leader yells "Go," the students are to quickly turn around and act out one of the phrases. For the gorilla, they make a gorilla stance and growl. For the gun, they point their finger and yell "bang." For karate, they are to strike a karate pose and yell "yaaa!" After they have done this, they look at the list to see who won. The losers sit and the winners find a new partner. This continues until there is one person left.

SPECIAL
FEATURES

NUMBER

PREP TIME

NONE

TIME REQUIRED

10 MINUTES

Grab Groups

HOW TO PLAY

Explain to the group that they will walk around and mingle until you yell out a number. They are then to form a group with that number of people in it. For example if you yell "Six!" they must stop and grab five other people to form small groups of six members each. When they do form the group of six, they are to sit down. If any group has more or less than six, they are out of the game and must sit on the sidelines. Then when you say, "Mingle" they start mingling again until the leader calls out another number, say three. This is repeated until there are only two people left.

Variation

You could expand on this idea by using this as a means to form discussion groups. These discussion groups could be formed to discuss just one topic or to form a group for a Bible study discussion. After calling out a number, ask them to sit down together to discuss a statement, verse or question. The topics could range from silly to serious. This can be used to discuss one topic, or after a few minutes of discussion, you could ask them to get up and mingle again until you call another number and give them another topic.

11/11/98

SPECIAL FEATURES

NUMBER

30+ PEOPLE

PREP TIME

NONE

TIME REQUIRED

10-15 MINUTES

CLEANUP LEVEL

The Head of Lettuce

MATERIALS NEEDED

A head of lettuce for every 12 to 15 students.

HOW TO PLAY

Divide the group into smaller groups of approximately of 12 to 15 students. Give each small group a fresh head of lettuce. Ask each student to carefully remove one entire leaf of lettuce and place it on the floor in front of them. Then pass the head of lettuce on to the next person who also removes a leaf. Continue around the circle until the head of lettuce is reduced to the heart. As the head goes around the circle, the leaves become smaller. As each student removes a leaf, he or she should keep it in the order of removal.

After the head has been completely disassembled, announce that now they need to reassemble the head of lettuce. Tell the students that when you shout "go," they should take the heart of the lettuce, place their leaf where it was, and pass it to the next person, until the head is reassembled.

Of course, this is impossible to accomplish since there is no pinning or gluing of the leaves back to the heart, but the point is to involve the students in an impossible, yet hilarious activity.

If any group decides to take this challenge seriously, the key to a level of success is in reassembling the head with great slowness, being careful in handing it off to the next person. This is a great way for the youth leaders to challenge the students to working together to solve a problem. Only the adults know the key—taking their time to do it right.

SPECIAL FEATURES

NUMBER

PREP TIME

NONE

TIME REQUIRED

10-15 MINUTES

Ice Cream Hunt

MATERIALS NEEDED

Five gift certificates from local ice cream or yogurt shop

PREPARATION

Have five students planted in the audience. Each plant will have a gift certificate for the local ice cream or frozen yogurt shop (or a similar prize).

HOW TO PLAY

Ask students to stand, walk around and mingle. When the agreed upon signal is given, have everyone stop where they are.

Have the first person with a gift certificate shout out "Here I am!" and then give a gift certificate to the person next to him or her. Have the students mingle again and repeat. Do this five times.

Middle Name Tags

MATERIALS NEEDED

Name tags
Felt-tip pens

HOW TO PLAY

Have everyone write their middle names on their name tags rather than their first and/or last names. If some are too embarrassed to do this, ask them to place their middle initial on the tag. Occasionally, some students will have no middle names, so ask them to give themselves one they would like.

Spend the rest of the meeting pointedly using as many middle names as possible. Require each student to refer to each other by middle names. Even have the students use their middle names when talking to you. You can set this up by repeatedly asking them, "What was your name again?"

SPECIAL FEATURES

NUMBER

PREP TIME

NONE

TIME REQUIRED

10 MINUTES

My Aunt Came Back

This is an audience participation song in which the joke is on the students! I know it's hard to teach a song without being there in person, but you can do it.

MATERIALS NEEDED

A copy of the song (if you don't have it memorized)

HOW TO PLAY

In this song the leader sings a line, and then acts out a motion and the audience mimics each line and motion. The results are hilarious.

The leader announces that this is a song that requires audience participation. The tune could be anything you want, just keep it really simple so the audience can repeat it easily.

Leader sings:	"My aunt came back..."
Audience:	"My aunt came back..."
Leader:	"From Kalamazoo."
Audience:	"From Kalamazoo."
Leader:	"She brought with her..."
Audience:	"She brought with her..."
Leader:	"Some gum to chew." *At this point begin making an exaggerated chewing motion as if you were chewing a huge piece of gum. The audience should do the same.*
Audience:	"Some gum to chew."

That was the first line of five lines. Sing each line and act out the motion with the audience repeating after you.

Line two:	"My aunt came back..." *Audience repeats.*
	"From New Orleans." *Audience repeats.*
	"She brought with her..." *Audience repeats.*
	"A pair of jeans." *Hit your hip with your hand and entice the audience to do the same. You and the audience should be chewing gum and hitting your hip all at the same time. Audience repeats.*
Line three:	"My aunt came back..." *Audience repeats.*

"From Niagara Falls." *Audience repeats.*

"She brought with her..." *Audience repeats.*

"Some ping-pong balls." *Sway left to right as if you where watching a ping-pong game being played (or as if you were playing ping-pong. Now, you and the audience should be chewing, hitting your hips, with your head swaying side to side. Audience repeats.*

Line four: "My aunt came back..." *Audience repeats.*

"From the New York Fair." *Audience repeats.*

"She brought with her..." *Audience repeats.*

"A rocking chair." *Now rock forward and back while, at the same time chewing, hitting your hips, and head swaying side to side. Audience repeats.*

Line five: "My aunt came back..." *Audience repeats.*

"From Timbuktu." *Audience repeats.*

"She brought with her..." *Audience repeats.*

"Some NUTS LIKE YOU!" *Point at the audience as you say this!*

Stop everything and point to the audience! The joke's on them!

SPECIAL FEATURES

NUMBER

PREP TIME

15-30 MINUTES

TIME REQUIRED

15 MINUTES

Name Tag Puzzle Match

MATERIALS NEEDED

Name tags
Felt-tip pens
Scissors

PREPARATION

Prior to the meeting, cut each name tag into two pieces, making different jagged, curved or zigzag cuts on each one. On the two pieces, write names that can be split into two parts, but share similar endings. For example, there are several famous superheroes whose names end in "man," "woman," " boy" or "girl" such as Superman, Wonder Woman, Spiderman, Batman and Bat Girl.

HOW TO PLAY

As the students gather, they each select a piece of name tag puzzle. When they find the person who matches with the other half, that person becomes their partner for the evening.

Variation

You could also use famous people who share the same last names. You can get names from collections of biographies. If the students don't know the name, it's okay because they can find the match by fitting the two puzzle pieces together.

One Match

MATERIALS NEEDED

A large box of wooden matches

HOW TO PLAY

Have the students sit in a circle and give a match to each student. One at a time, each student will light his or her match, then name off as many facts about him- or herself before the match burns out, or he or she blows it out.

If you have a group of 20 or more, have students form smaller groups of 8 to 10 to do this activity.

5/26/99

Onion Toss

MATERIALS NEEDED

A peeled onion
A tape or CD player or musical instrument
Music to play

HOW TO PLAY

Have the group sit down in a circle. Another person needs to control the music source—a tape or CD player or a musical instrument. In all fairness the person playing the music should not be able to see who has the onion.

Tell the group that while the music is playing an onion is going to be passed around the circle. When the music stops, the person who is left holding the onion must take a bite. After the bite has been taken, the music begins and the onion is tossed again, and the process starts all over. Do this six or eight times.

Partners

SPECIAL FEATURES

NUMBER

PREP TIME

NONE

TIME REQUIRED

10-15 MINUTES

HOW TO PLAY

Have each student choose a partner. Have each pair stand back-to-back. On the count of three, instruct them to turn around and do one of the following contests (leader's choice):

- Each partner indicates a number with his or her fingers, then they each add the numbers. First one to add correctly wins and finds a new partner. The losers sit down on the sidelines.
- Each partner indicates a number with his or her fingers, then they each multiply the numbers. First one finished wins. The losers sit down on the sidelines.
- Each partner indicates a number with his or her fingers, then they each subtract the difference between the numbers. First one finished wins. The losers sit down on the sidelines
- Have them turn quickly, face each other and play a thumb war. The losers sit down on the sidelines.

Eliminate the losers each time and have students form pairs with new partners until there is only one student left.

Roll Sharing

MATERIALS NEEDED

A roll or two of toilet paper (depending on the size of the group)

HOW TO PLAY

Have students form a circle, either standing or sitting. Pass around a roll of toilet paper, telling the students, "Take any number of pieces of toilet paper up to ten pieces." Give no further instructions.

After everyone has their sheets of toilet paper, announce that for every sheet of toilet paper each group member has selected, he or she must share something about him- or herself that other group members don't know. As each person shares one thing, he or she rips off one piece of toilet paper and throws it into the center. This activity works best if each student shares only one piece of information at a time, giving students a chance to build on the other students' ideas and stories.

Scar Show and Tell

SPECIAL FEATURES

NUMBER

PREP TIME

NONE

TIME REQUIRED

10 MINUTES

HOW TO PLAY

Have group members show and tell their war stories about the scars that they *can* show to everyone in the room. Sharing the stories of wounds can be a very meaningful, even emotional time. It can also be simply goofy because many of our scars are due to silly mistakes. Whatever the reason, these little, brief times of sharing help students to know more about one another and thus promote a sense of unity and a we-are-in-this-life-together attitude.

SPECIAL
FEATURES

NUMBER

PREP TIME

10-15 MINUTES

TIME REQUIRED

15-20 MINUTES

CLEANUP LEVEL

REQUIREMENTS

Snowball Fight

MATERIALS NEEDED

Volleyball net or long rope
Bedsheets, tarps or painters' dropcloths
A large amount of newspapers (collected ahead of time)

PREPARATION

Begin to collect the newspapers a few weeks before you do this activity. Divide the playing area by stringing a volleyball net or long rope across the center. The divider should only be about three or four feet high. Drape bedsheets or other large pieces of cloth over the net (or rope) so that the two teams cannot see each other when seated on the floor or ground.

HOW TO PLAY

Divide your group into two equal teams. Have them sit on opposite sides of the draped net, or rope.

Give each group a large stack of newspapers and tell them they are going to have a snowball fight. On the signal from you, tell them to begin wadding up newspaper "snowballs" and throw the snowballs at the other team. After a few minutes, stop the action and decide which team has the least amount of paper snowballs on its side of the net—that team wins (or, if you're doing this several times, give that team a point). Continue this as long as time allows or when one team reaches a certain score.

S'prees!

SPECIAL FEATURES

NUMBER

PREP TIME

NONE

TIME REQUIRED

10-15 MINUTES

MATERIALS NEEDED

A large bag of M&Ms, Skittles or other multi-colored candy

HOW TO PLAY

Give everyone an M&M, Skittle, or other multi-colored candy as they walk in the door. Tell them to memorize their colors and then eat the candy. After everyone has arrived, explain the game.

Tell them that when all of the lights go out, they are to yell out their color and find as many other people with their color as they can and form a group by interlocking arms.

Turn off the lights quickly before they have time to begin looking for friends and asking them their color. After a few minutes, turn the lights back on and see which group is the largest. The chaos is wild and crazy fun.

SPECIAL FEATURES

NUMBER

10+ PEOPLE

PREP TIME

NONE

TIME REQUIRED

10 MINUTES

Toss Up

HOW TO PLAY

Have the group form smaller groups of 5 to 10 members. However, all groups must have the same number of students.

Here's what they do: One person in each group lies down, and the rest of the group picks that person up and throws him or her into the air *and* catches the person. Then have them do the same thing to each person in their small group. They continue until everyone in the group has been thrown into the air and caught. First group to finish throwing each person wins.

Note: Advise students to do this activity in a reasonable manner so that no one is hurt.

Touch

SPECIAL FEATURES

NUMBER

PREP TIME

NONE

TIME REQUIRED

10 MINUTES

PREPARATION

Remove any obstacles or anything that is breakable from the play area.

HOW TO PLAY

Have everyone line up in one straight line down the middle of your room. Have the other adult leaders stand around to judge which student is last and whether or not each student gets back into line correctly.

Instruct the group that you will call out an object or place and when you say "Go," they are to run and touch that object or place. For example, you might say, "Touch the front door. Go!" then everyone runs and touches the front door and then runs back to their same place in line.

The last student to make it back into his or her spot is out. Continue this until there is only one student left.

The following are some examples of objects or places to use:

- Touch Jim's hat.
- Touch Pastor Bob.
- Touch Mary's foot
- Touch the back door *and* the ping-pong table.

SPECIAL
FEATURES

NUMBER

PREP TIME

NONE

TIME REQUIRED

10-15 MINUTES

Towel Toss

This is an active icebreaker, especially for younger students.

MATERIALS NEEDED

A towel

HOW TO PLAY

Have the whole group form one huge circle and sit down. Select one student to sit in the middle who is It. Give the towel to one of the students sitting in the circle. When you say go, It is to try and get the towel or touch one of the people who is holding the towel while everyone in the circle tries their best to get rid of the towel by throwing it around the circle. If the person in the middle catches the towel, the person who threw it is now It.

This is a fast, action-packed game and can last for any length of time you choose.

Variations

You can also add variations such as using two towels, or a ball and a towel, or a ball and a shirt. Use your imagination!

Trains

This works best with large groups; in fact, the larger the better.

HOW TO PLAY

Have the group form a large circle. Choose three or four leaders who will be "the Engines" to begin. These "Engines" each chugga-chugga-chug to another person in the circle, grab him or her by the shoulders and ask his or her name. When the person says his or her name, the Engine hops on one leg and say the person's name. Then, the Engine hops on the other leg and says the person's name. He or she does this a total of five hops on each leg.

After the fifth time, the two people form a two-person train with the new person becoming the Engine at the front and the other person holding on to the shoulders of the new Engine. The trains will each move to another student in the circle. Repeat the process: ask the person's name, say the name while hopping five times, and the new person becomes the Engine of the train each time. After a few minutes, huge trains of students are formed, running around and through each other.

SPECIAL FEATURES

NUMBER

PREP TIME

NONE

TIME REQUIRED

10-15 MINUTES

Trivial Pursuit Warm-Up

This activity makes a good transition between a rowdy time and a quieter time such as between game time and Bible study.

MATERIALS NEEDED

Trivial Pursuit question cards
Small pieces of candy
Three large candy bars

PREPARATION

Choose at least nine Trivial Pursuit question cards (or more if you have the time) ahead of time. You will use two as "practice questions" and one as a "winner question." The practice questions should be a little easier (and hopefully a little bizarre). After the two practice cards, select a "winner question" which should be more difficult and hopefully even a little more bizarre.

HOW TO PLAY

Tell students they are going to play Trivial Pursuit. You will read two practice questions and whoever shouts out the correct answer gets a piece of candy (or other small treat) thrown to them. After completing the first two practice questions, inform them that you will now read the winning question and whoever shouts out the correct answer gets a full-size candy bar (or team points). Continue to alternate: two practice questions, one winner question; two practice, one winner, etc.

   Tip: This would also be a good activity around a heavy academic time of the school year for the students such as during finals or when school is about to start.

What Matches?

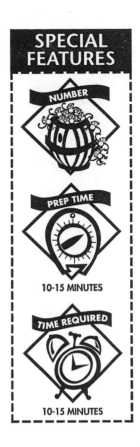

SPECIAL
FEATURES

NUMBER

PREP TIME

10-15 MINUTES

TIME REQUIRED

10-15 MINUTES

MATERIALS NEEDED

Chalkboard, white board, overhead projector and transparency, or sheet of newsprint

PREPARATION

Write on the board, an overhead transparency or on a sheet of newsprint the following statements:

- Who I am, really.
- Who others seem to think I am.
- My most important goal.

HOW TO PLAY

As the students gather, tell them that they will be paired up in various ways and share their answers to the three questions in several different groups of people. To get them to mix, prepare a number of criteria. For example, have them find one other person...

- With the same color of pants/skirt or shirt/top
- With or without words printed on their T-shirts
- With the same number of rings on
- Wearing the same amount or kinds of jewelry
- With or without braces
- With or without glasses
- With the same hair color
- In the same grade level in school
- With the same favorite soda flavor
- With the same favorite sport
- With or without toenail polish color

Call out a category and watch to see that the students pair up with one other person who meets the criteria. If you have uneven numbers, allow three people to team up. Then have them share their responses to the three questions with each other. When everyone has shared, call out a new category and have them find a new partner and exchange responses.

What's Important?

This crowdbreaker will always illicit total participation from the students. It has never failed to create the feelings it is designed to create.

SPECIAL FEATURES

NUMBER

PREP TIME

NONE

TIME REQUIRED

15-20 MINUTES

MATERIALS NEEDED

A large quantity of 3x5-inch index cards or slips of paper,
   10 per person
Pens or pencils

HOW TO PLAY

1. Have everyone sit in a large circle, preferably on the floor. Give everyone in the room ten 3x5-inch index cards (or slips of paper) and a pen or pencil.

2. Have everyone write the ten most important things in their life, one item per card: i.e. my family, God, my dog, my Bible, my health, etc. You can prime their thoughts with a few suggestions.

3. When they are done writing on the cards, have them turn their cards face down and shuffle them so that they have no idea which cards are where in the stack. **Very important:** Do not let them look at what is written on the cards once they are shuffled.

4. Say something like, "Martians have just come into our town. They come to your homes and hold each of you at laser gunpoint, demanding that you give up the top three cards on your stack. Without looking at them, pull off the top three cards. You no longer have these things. The Martians have taken them from you." There will be many moans and groans from the youth, and they will not want to give up some of the things that the Martians have taken from them. Have them read their cards to themselves as they throw the cards one at a time into the center of the circle. Ask them to take a look at the seven items they still have.

5. Say something like, "Just when you are getting over the shock of the loss of those three things, a roving band of Plutonians come to your door. They demand money from you, but you have none. They say, 'Give us two items of your choice, and we won't torch your house!' Now, looking at the cards remaining, pick out two of

them (your choice) and throw them into the middle of the room. After you give them your two items, they leave you alone." Now, have them shuffle the cards face down once again.

6. Keep going along these same lines, alternating back and forth between discarding cards according to choice or without looking at the cards. Make up another story each time (natural disasters, burglars, etc.). Stop when students each have only two cards left, then make them choose between the two.

APPLICATION

There are a number of different directions this activity can lead. It can be used as a springboard for a discussion on priorities or on the illusion of the control we have over our own lives, or how cushy our lives are compared to people in the rest of the world. This activity can result in the students exploring what it feels like to experience disastrous loss. There are groans of anguish as the students struggle with losing the things listed on their cards. It also helps them take a look at what has lasting value over things that are less important.

Where I've Been

MATERIALS NEEDED

Several maps of the United States/the world, one map for
   about 10 students
Straight pins or push pins
Small slips of paper
Paper
Pens or pencils

PREPARATION

Attach the maps to walls around the room.

HOW TO PLAY

Give each student ten straight pins or push pins, a pen or pencil, and
10 slips of paper. Tell students to write their names on their ten slips
of paper, then stick a pin through the end of each tag.

Have students pair up and talk about their travels with their partners. They can describe their favorite vacation spot, the most exotic
location, the farthest trip, the longest, most boring trip, etc. After they
share with their partners, they list their top 10 favorite places. Have the
pairs team up with four other pairs to form groups of ten. Have each
group of ten gather around one of the maps taped to the walls around
the room. After everyone has made their lists, have each person push
the pins with their names attached into the maps to show how much
and how far group members have traveled.

This activity can lead into the topic of world evangelism, or similar
topics relevant to the call of the Church to go into the world and share
their faith in Christ.

To close, form a prayer circle and lead the students in praying for
those people they met on their trips and to challenge them to see their
future travels as opportunities for sharing the Good News throughout
the world.

Who Am I?

This is a great game to get students to mingle.

MATERIALS NEEDED

Sticky notes or small slips of paper

PREPARATION

On the sticky notes or slips of paper, write the names of several characters from cartoons, TV shows, movies, books, the Bible or any other similar source that can provide you with well-known characters. Have enough for one for every group member.

HOW TO PLAY

As group members arrive, stick the notes (or pin the slips of paper) on each person's back so that he or she cannot see the name. The object of the game is for each person to figure out who he or she is by asking other members yes or no questions about his or her character.

For example, if the category is TV shows, they will want to begin by asking general questions: "Am I in a cartoon?" "Am I on a sitcom?" "Am I a male (female) character?" When they guess their names correctly, have them give you the piece of paper. Then they continue to help others find out who they really are. Limit the time to about 10 minutes or less.

SPECIAL FEATURES

NUMBER

PREP TIME

15-30 MINUTES

TIME REQUIRED

10-15 MINUTES

Word of the Week

This fun icebreaker is a real "moaner."

MATERIALS NEEDED

Chalk or white board, poster board, or overhead projector and transparency
Appropriate writing instrument
Wild clothing and props for a crazy costume

PREPARATION

Select someone—student or adult—to become your Word Wizard, Word Nerd, or other silly name. Dress this person as a wacky character (i.e., a nutty professor with a commencement robe and mortarboard, a nerdy person, a crazy magician, etc.). Give this person the word list so he or she can prepare each week.

HOW TO PLAY

Tell the whole group that you have brought in an expert to help them with their SAT scores and you are beginning a new program for them called the "Word of the Week." Introduce your guest, then he or she comes forward and introduces this week's word.

Have him or her do each of the following:

1. Write the Word of the Week on the board, a piece of poster board or an overhead transparency.
2. Define it.
3. Use it in a sentence. For example: "Today's word is 'gorilla.' Gorilla means 'to cook by gentle heating.' " A sample sentence: "Honey, will you please make me a *gorilla* cheese sandwich?"

Tip: Be sure to use *the* Word of the Week in the sample sentence. For example: Do not say "grilled" instead of "gorilla" because that would ruin the absurdity of the joke. Also, continue the Word of the Week activity for several weeks.

OTHER WORDS OF THE WEEK

- Declare—"cloudlessness" (the clear)
- Diploma—"one who fixes the sink" (the plumber)
- Enunciate—"what gave the cannibal an upset stomach" (a nun she ate)
- Europe—"out of bed early" (you're up)
- European—"an insult" (you're a pain)
- Excel—"the price of eggs" (eggs sell)
- Granite—"to disregard or forget about" (granted)
- Gruesome— "to grow in size or number" (grew some)
- Handsome—"to pass along" (hand some)
- Harmonious—"location of our funds" (our money is)
- Intense—"where we sleep on a camping trip" (in tents)
- Isolate—"excuse for not being on time" (I so late)
- Khaki—"small metal object that starts a car" (car key)
- Officiate—"seafood eaten" (a fish he ate)
- Token—"speaking" (talking)

Community Builders

community \kə-'myü-nə-te\ *n, pl* **-ties 1** : a unified body of individuals: as **a** : STATE, COMMONWEALTH **b** : the people with common interests living in a particular area **c** : an interacting population of various kinds of individuals (as species) in a common location **3 a** : joint ownership or participation **b** : common character: LIKENESS <of interests> **c** : social activity: FELLOWSHIP
builder \'bil-dər\ *n* (13c) **1** : one that builds; *esp* : one that contracts to build and supervises building operations **2** : a substance added to or used with detergents to increase their cleansing action (from *Merriam Webster's Collegiate Dictionary, Tenth Edition*).

A community builder is any activity that promotes the deeper sense of the group among its members. Some are brief and used to encourage the development of ongoing relationships. Some are longer, having a specific goal in mind. One takes the entire year to do correctly, involving a few minutes at each meeting.

Visitors need an opportunity to become part of the group as soon as possible, so we have chosen community builders that groups of any size can use. Longtime members need to know that they continue to have an important part in the group. Younger students just entering the group need some assurance that they are accepted. Community-building activities are great for accomplishing all of these goals.

Special thanks to whoever it was out there in ministryland that dreamed up these gems. To each of you originators, I tip my hat and assure you that if I knew who you were, I'd give you full credit.

—Mark Simone

Alternative Popularity Contest

This activity is longer than most and takes planning. It will occupy a whole meeting, requiring about an hour for a group of 30 to complete. It also needs to include a game or snack break. However, it is well worth the time and preparation.

Traditionally, the measures of teenage popularity have been attached to scholastic or athletic ability, good looks, best clothing sense and other superficial criteria. Admittedly, these standards leave many, if not most, teenagers on the outside looking in at the popular circles.

The usual criteria for popularity represent only a fraction of the total abilities that can be found in any group of people. So to break the molds and spotlight all of the students in your group, try an Alternative Popularity Contest.

MATERIALS NEEDED

Photocopies of ballots
Pens or pencils
Nomination sheets
Transparent/masking tape or several tables
Ballot containers for each category (small boxes or baskets)

PREPARATION

Advertise that in this meeting, everyone will have a chance to be recognized by their peers for the great gifts God has given each one. Brainstorm with other adult leaders, or through contacting parents, many categories of giftedness that are found among the youth group members. See the list of possible suggestions that follows these directions.

Prepare ballots with categories ahead of time and photocopy enough for everyone. Also prepare blank ballots for write-in nominations. Also prepare a sign-in sheet for all students to sign as they enter the meeting (so adult leaders can make sure each student receives an award).

WHAT TO DO

Here are the steps to the process:

- You'll need lots of ballots and pens or pencils. Each category will be posted on the nomination sheets hung on the walls or placed on tables around the room. List the category in large print at the top of the sheet. Each voter will write his or her nomination for each category on these nomination sheets. The nomination sheets look best when produced with a computer, but handwritten nomination categories will work just fine. Extra blank sheets need to be provided for added category ideas.

- Nominating occurs when each student reads a category and then nominates one person for each category. Each participant should walk from sheet to sheet, deciding who to choose for each category, and write one nomination for each category. Place ballots in a container located under each category sheet.

- Have other adult leaders tally the votes and award the title to the candidate with the most votes. Each student should only win one award. When someone wins a category, record his or her name on a list to be announced later. The goal will be to make sure that every student in attendance gets an award. Therefore, the advisors will need to be aware of what is going on and have some categories ready to add, and give credit to the ones who may be overlooked. However, if you plan the program well, every student gets nominated for something.

- Have a standard certificate ready and fill it in, noting the winner's name and the category. Put some strongly affirming language in a certificate similar to the one on page 170.

HOW TO BEGIN

When the group is assembled, tell them,

> Each of us is a special creation of God. In his limitless variety, God has made us a unique blend of gifts and attributes unique on the planet. Unfortunately, our society focuses on only a very few of the more superficial measures of popularity: the size and shape of our bodies, our looks, hairstyle, sports, clothes, grades and the like. However, tonight we will be recognizing and awarding other types of achievement. On with the show!

Then instruct the students in how to do the voting.

Distribute pens or pencils and let the students walk around and browse the categories. They may nominate themselves or a friend for any listed category. With advisor approval, they may add a new category for nominations.

After nominations are closed, the students will vote (one vote per nomination category). Adult leaders count the votes where the students cannot see them and they make a list with a winner for each category. Provide a snack, game time or other activity while the counting is being done. Advisors should list only one person per category. Don't allow multiple winners. Also, they should check the winners with the sign-in sheet to make sure each student receives an award. If a student wins in more than one category, choose the most appropriate one to award that student. Then award the other categories to the second- or third-place nominees. In other words, if Jane has won three different awards, give her the category most befitting her, and award the other two categories to someone else who was nominated but did not have the most votes. It is much easier than it sounds!

Complete the event with a lavish awards ceremony with lots of affirmations and applause. Close with a prayer circle thanking God for investing so much in each person, and for allowing everyone to grow together as a group.

Suggested Categories

Best joke teller

Most interesting dresser

Best bargain shopper

Knows the most trivia

Most active in worship

Biggest sports fan

Greatest animal lover

Best musician

Most volunteerism at church

Best evangelist

Most community service

Best natural comic ability

Best laugh

Most fitting name

Kindest

Fastest talker

Greatest knowledge of Scripture

Most colorful clothing

Cleanest car

Most artistic

Owns the most hats

Most adventuresome

Newest to the youth group

Strongest witness for Christ

Best storyteller

Hardest worker

Best cook

Quickest with a quip or comeback

Always smells good

Best hairdo

Friendliest

Safest driver

Most athletic	Most courageous
Asks the best questions	Greatest technology expert
Best singer	Most positive
Most Christlike servant	Most helpful
Most joyful	Most honest
Most compassionate	Most generous
Best businessperson	Most inventive

Try to focus on positive attributes, and tailor-make plenty of categories to fit your group.

You Are Special!

_____,

recognizing that you are blessed with many good attributes and specially gifted by God, you have been chosen by your fellow youth group members and leaders to be especially honored for your special gift of

_____

On this day _____

Signed _____

An "It's-Not-My Birthday!" Birthday

When on the road for mission trips or work camps, it's fun to treat the students to at least one nice meal—usually in a fun place such as a Hard Rock Cafe or a Planet Hollywood-type restaurant. After the meal, honor one of the older students—usually one who is graduating and will soon be heading away to college—with a birthday cake and "Happy Birthday" sung to them by the servers. Of course, make sure that the honoree's actual birthday is a few months away, and never give clues as to who the target will be.

It is one of those affirming fun things that long remain in the memories of the whole group. It becomes a strong group builder because it is just one of those wild things to look forward to. It also lends itself to the community spirit of fun on trips. The honorees always feel a degree of honor (after they recover from the slight embarrassment) so you may want to pick one of the more peripheral students who may not have shone as brightly as some of the youth group stars. It can become a badge of great recognition to be picked.

Curriculum Creations

SPECIAL FEATURES

NUMBER

8+ PEOPLE

PREP TIME

30+ MINUTES

TIME REQUIRED

60 MINUTES

This community builder requires a few weeks to come to completion. Do not be afraid to dedicate a month's worth of meetings to the program. It will develop relationships and leadership among small groups, who in turn will share their creation with the larger group.

MATERIALS NEEDED

Old Sunday School/youth ministry curriculum
Scissors
Transparent tape/glue
Pens and pencils
Paper
Felt-tip pens
Newsprint

PREPARATION

Prior to the first week that you do this activity, gather as much old Sunday School and youth ministry curriculum as you can. Anything from decades ago up to the previous year will do.

Gather all of the supplies on tables in the middle of the youth group meeting area.

WHAT TO DO

Divide students into small groups of four to seven members. Tell them that they have the assignment of developing a youth group meeting that they will lead in the weeks to come. Help them to understand the various elements of the meetings they will lead. Let them mix up the order or change some elements if they want.

You may want to suggest something like the following outline:
- Opening activity (a game or icebreaker)
- Worship/Music
- Introduction activity for study
- The Bible lesson/study
- Discussion
- Wrap-up
- Snack
- Closing prayer

Add or delete any other elements that you use or don't use.

Instruct the students to go through the curricula to find things to use in developing any kind of meeting they wish with the catch that in the coming weeks they will lead the meeting they have created.

Most of the students, if not all, will take the assignment very seriously. Do not interpret attempts at being creative with cutting up. Some groups, if they get in a jam, may try to act like they don't care or goof off to cover their frustrations or embarrassment. Be ready to help interpret, support, bail out or modify. Let them know you are available to advise when they have a problem, but avoid working out their difficulties for them.

This activity has promise on so many levels. Don't be afraid to try it! Some of the benefits may be that they will have a better appreciation for the difficulty of your job, you may gain some insight into what interests them and new group leaders may be developed in the process.

SPECIAL FEATURES

NUMBER

PREP TIME

5-10 MINUTES

TIME REQUIRED

N/A

E-Mail Prayer List

Authorities tell us that teenagers around the country are logging zillions of hours on the Internet. While this packs its own concerns for us, it may also hold some uncharted possibilities.

MATERIALS NEEDED

Computers with on-line service

WHAT TO DO

Establish an on-line prayer concerns list to be E-mailed to the addresses of your youth group members. When you hear of a need, post it for all of the students who are on-line. The hope is that they will read it, pray for the needy person, then log a response to him or her or to other group members. Eventually the students will begin posting their own entries and concerns.

It is important to check the mail every day or so to make sure you as the initiator are aware of what the students are posting. Not because of bad stuff, but because they will need to know you, too, are using the E-mail and praying for them.

This is also a somewhat anonymous way for quiet students who never ask for prayer to make their needs for prayer known to others.

You may need to educate your on-line students on the use of the E-mail address book and how they can post a note to everyone in the group who is on-line.

Freshmen No More

SPECIAL FEATURES

NUMBER

PREP TIME

10 MINUTES

TIME REQUIRED

60+ MINUTES

It is hard to get away from identifying students in a high school group apart from their grade level. Yet for younger students especially, acceptance as an equal is a very important factor in feeling like a part of the group. At school the freshmen are often the focus of unkind jokes, pranks or comments. Many feel insecurity, or even terror, at leaving middle or junior high school for the perils of high school.

The youth group needs to be a very welcoming and comforting place for freshmen. Yet, if they are referred to as freshmen, the impression is still that they are not part of the group, or at least that they are on probation for a year before being fully accepted.

In your first meeting or activity at which the freshmen join the youth group for the first time, divide all of the students into the four corners of the room by grade. Beginning with the seniors, introduce each person and applaud the whole bunch. Then the juniors, sophomores, and finally the freshmen.

Then ask the other three grades to mingle with the freshmen, learn names, introduce themselves and personally welcome each new student. After this mingling has happened, have each older student pick a freshman as his or her guest for the evening and eat a meal together.

Games follow, maybe a brief Bible devotion, and other features such as reviewing the coming year's schedule and making announcements.

At the end of the evening, have all of the freshmen stand inside a circle of the older students and have a prayer of thanksgiving to God for blessing your group with such a wonderfully gifted set of new members. Then give the following announcement:

> Tonight you came to us as freshmen. You are new to our group and there are still some things we need to share with you and that you need to share with us. In the months to come, we are going to get to know you better. We'll learn your names and what you like to do. We'll go on trips together and study God's Word with you. But that is hard to do if we all look at you as underclassmen. In Christ there is no east or west, no male and female and no class divisions. We are all His children. Therefore, from this night on, you will no longer be called freshmen. The name is gone. From now on, you are our sisters and brothers in Christ and an important

part of this group. The designation of freshman is gone. Welcome to youth group.

This is even more impressive if a senior or junior says it. How many of those freshmen do you think will be back next week? And how many of them will want to bring a friend?

giG

SPECIAL FEATURES

NUMBER

PREP TIME

5-15 MINUTES

TIME REQUIRED

60+ MINUTES

For the most part, any high school group functions very well as a large group. But there are problems, at times, with different ages understanding the challenges of a student just entering high school and one about to graduate. Some of the older students quit participating in youth group because they cannot relate to the younger students who seem so immature to them.

In one youth group that is called GROUP, the youth pastor called a meeting of the eleventh and twelfth graders to decide what they could do. The youth pastor told them their leadership and experience were needed as an example of maturity for the younger students. He proposed a second meeting, which meets twice a month, that eventually became "group in GROUP" or giG. giG works, and has in some ways revolutionized the youth ministry. As a community building experience, it has strengthened the relationships of the older students with the younger, as well as the youth leader's relationship with all the students.

At giG the group discusses issues more relevant to the lives of those looking at graduation and college. They meet to discuss a proposed topic or agenda, and then the youth leader lets the students' discussions meander as they please, just as long as they remain relevant or important to their faith and walk with Christ. The group meets in homes, which seems to encourage more openness.

This model is highly recommended for any moderate to large-sized youth program.

Gratitude Pictures

This activity takes about an hour to an hour and a half.

MATERIALS NEEDED

> Several 9x12-inch sheets of colored construction paper, one
> sheet per student
> Several pairs of scissors
> Several bottles of glue, or glue sticks
> A large stack of old magazines
> A small slip of paper for each student
> A box or similar container, to hold slips of paper

HOW TO PLAY

As the students gather have each of them write their names on slips of paper and put them into a box, hat or other similar container. When the meeting begins, have everyone choose a name from the container. Instruct them that they are to keep the name they chose to themselves.

Tell students they will cut or tear pictures from the magazines that describe the person whose name they picked. If anyone is stymied by the name picked because he or she doesn't know the person at all, he or she may trade for another name with the help of the advisors. In that situation it is best to gather several of the names and have several students redraw names.

The students should note the great, wonderful, unique, gifted things about the person as they chose pictures or words from the magazines. The aim is to thank God through illustrative affirmations about the person being depicted.

The activity becomes a guessing game when the whole group is invited to figure out who is being portrayed. Each "artist" may point out what is being depicted about the person.

If visitors are in attendance, the person bringing the visitor may need to trade names with the guest so that he or she is not left out.

Human Bingo

MATERIALS NEEDED

Photocopies of your customized Bingo sheets
Pens or pencils

PREPARATION

Customize the Bingo sheet to make it appropriate for your group. By choosing 16 items, questions, experiences or statements relevant to your area, it's a sure way to mix the students up and build community as they mingle to gather signatures.

At the top of each of the four-by-four squares write various common or wacky questions to ask the participants. The items in the squares may focus on the Bible study topic for that meeting, or on school, family, church, faith, sports, fun activities or any other theme. As you put it together, think about what is relevant to the current or recent experiences of the teenagers in your group or area.

HOW TO PLAY

Tell students they are to collect signatures of other group members who fit into each of the Bingo categories. Set a time limit for them to gather signatures—less than ten minutes is best. When time is up, collect the sheets and have another youth worker decide the winner. The first to complete the whole sheet or to have the most rows or columns completed is the winner. Rather than a time limit, you could have the first one to complete two rows or columns or the whole sheet shout BINGO!

Some might consider Human Bingo an icebreaker, but anytime teenagers are discovering this much information about one another, you're building community.

Pages 181-182 contain a sample Bingo sheet and a blank Bingo sheet for you to copy. The categories at the top of each column are optional.

Variation

Assign a category to each of the four columns: i.e., My Favorite Sport, My Worst Color, The Food I Love, My Dream Vacation. Then have each student write his or her own response in the first square under each category. When they have completed that step, give them a time limit, say five to seven minutes, to find other group members with the same or similar answers to sign the three squares below each of their answers.

Human Bingo

Collect one signature for each square. Signatures must include both the first and last names.

Leisure Activities	Personal	Likes & Dislikes	Miscellaneous
Hasn't watched TV in over two days	Has both a brother and a sister	Is radically committed to Jesus	Someone who is wearing something with a school logo
Has been snow skiing during the past year	Does NOT snore!	Loves to sing	Has his or her own car
Plays basketball on a school team	New to our group in the last month	Likes to eat broccoli	Has had their house *TP*ed
Plays a musical instrument	Sings in the shower	Hates Rap music	Has his or her own telephone number

Human Bingo

Collect one signature for each square. Signatures must include both the first and last names.

Indoor Campout

This event is a blast when the winter months set in and your students get cabin fever. It works as an all-day activity, an overnighter or a long meeting. The more time spent on the activity, the better the effect. So when the students get stir crazy, nothing helps more than an Indoor Campout that involves them in games, singing, sharing, food and all the rest of the things we love about camping.

MATERIALS NEEDED

> A few tents
> Artificial/real trees and plants
> Sleeping bags
> Rocks, fireplace logs, red spotlight or red cellophane (for
>   fake campfire)

PREPARING THE CAMP ATMOSPHERE

The first step in having a successful Indoor Campout is to create the right atmosphere. Generally people go camping in the forest in tents. Therefore, your goal will be to create a forest and provide tents for your students. Surprisingly, a forest is not hard to create. Many people today have artificial Christmas trees stored in the attic. Borrow as many as you can from church families or ask large department stores to let you use their display Christmas trees. Set up the trees in your youth room or fellowship hall. Put the trees in groupings of three or so with varying heights. Also collect artificial or real potted plants to add to the outdoor feeling.

Borrow some tents as well. You will not have to have enough tents for all of the students because they will not be sleeping in them. However, you do need enough to create the feel of a campsite.

Other props and accessories that can be used to create atmosphere are fake snow, stuffed animals, the sound of running water and singing birds, and a campfire. Of course, it's not recommended that you start a real fire in your church! A realistic campfire can be made from a circle of stones, some real pieces of wood and a red spot light or red cellophane paper.

CAMPING GAMES

Generally a camping theme can be integrated into your usual favorite games and activities. See pages 28-30 in the Games section of this book for the directions for the following:

1. Tent Relay
2. Pin the Tail on the Bear
3. Sleeping Bag Relay
4. Use your creativity to adapt other games to the camping theme.

CAMP FOOD

Food can also follow the camping theme. Make stew or spaghetti. Hot dogs or hamburgers are also appropriate. S'mores and mountain pies (pie filling cooked between pieces of bread) are common camping desserts that can be made in a conventional or microwave oven or indoor grill.

CAMPFIRE SONGS AND SHARING

You can't go camping without singing camp songs around the fire. Pick your favorites, find a guitar player and enjoy yourself! You could have a time of testimony around the "fire." Present a youth talk about commitment and open up a time for sharing.

The success of this activity is not so much the specifics of the camping atmosphere as it is a vehicle through which your group can become closer. Using the novel theme of indoor camping, nearly any topic can be adapted into a fun experience, and it is guaranteed to keep the attention of your students.

Let Us Bake Bread Together

If your group does day-long planning sessions, you can mix the planning with a great mission project.

MATERIALS NEEDED

> Several bread-making machines
> Ingredients needed for making bread (check machine recipes)

PREPARATION

Borrow as many bread-making machines as you can and provide enough ingredients to make a loaf of bread in each of the machines.

WHAT TO DO

Before the planning or leadership activity, assemble the group and have them combine the ingredients and put them in the bread-making machines. While the bread is baking, have your planning meeting. Most machines take three to four hours to bake a loaf so you'll have plenty of time to plan.

When the bread is baked, harvest your labors, clean the kitchen and deliver the bread to someone in your church, such as new members, the ill or the elderly. This is a good way to build rapport, underscore the concept of missions, and give the students an opportunity to start and finish a project together—all of which build community unity.

This might also be an opportunity to discuss the significance of bread in Communion or various references to the symbolism of bread in the New Testament.

SPECIAL FEATURES

NUMBER

PREP TIME

15 MINUTES

TIME REQUIRED

30 MINUTES

CLEANUP LEVEL

REQUIREMENTS

The Lost Civilization

One idea for a great small group builder is to have the group develop conclusions together about what the future archeologists and sociologists will think about their culture.

MATERIALS NEEDED

Paper
Pens or pencils

HOW TO PLAY

Divide students into four or five small groups. More are fine if your group is large. Ideally, there should be 5 to 10 students per group. Give the groups the following information:

> Tonight you will create a reality that will be interpreted by a group of searching archeologists from the year A.D. 2200 as they discover this area. Each group's members are permitted to wander around the church and each person is to bring back an item that represents our group/culture. You may bring anything you can carry that is not obviously going to get us in trouble. You may also gather things from outside the building. Assemble your things in an interesting display in the center of your meeting room. Then create a story that describes how you use these gathered symbols or items. Write down the story and return to this room.

Assign a room or area of a room to each small group for gathering their items and writing their story. Give the groups a time limit to complete their display and their story—about 30 to 45 minutes should be plenty of time. When the groups have collected and arranged their objects and written their stories, have them return to your meeting area.

The adult advisors will then lead the groups on a tour of ancient remains of a recently discovered lost civilization. Supply each of your advisor archeologists with a cap or distinctive hat, a magnifying glass and other campy uniform decorations. Lead the whole group from

room to room and interpret the collected artifacts. Utilize humor, past history courses, folklore or whatever to explain each collection. Then, after you have summed it all up, read newly discovered manuscripts—their written explanations—and see how close your conclusions about their displays were.

This activity builds camaraderie as the groups put their stories together and as their findings are discussed by the whole group.

SPECIAL FEATURES

NUMBER

PREP TIME

30-60 MINUTES

TIME REQUIRED

60 MINUTES

Love Songs

For this activity you will need access to a fairly large activity room.

MATERIALS NEEDED

Several blank cassette tapes
Several tape players
Paper
Pens or pencils
Transparent tape

PREPARATION

Before the meeting, tape parts of several songs on separate cassette tapes. Select from contemporary pop songs, standards, oldies or other music that the students will recognize. The songs should say something about love. Also select one good Christian song that has a love theme. Put the tapes and tape players in different locations around the meeting place. If space is small or if you want, you could place the tape players in various places around the church.

Prepare a copy of the questions and make photocopies to tape above or next to the tape players.

At the last station, have a taped reading of 1 Corinthians 13. It might be a good idea to have a written version that goes along with the tape, posted above the tape for both visual and audio emphasis.

WHAT TO DO

At the beginning of the meeting, have the students divide into groups of three or four. Have each group begin at a different tape player station. Tell them to listen to the tape at each station and discuss their answers to the following questions (have the questions photocopied and taped above or next to each tape player):

- What does the song say about love?
- What is the attitude of the songwriter towards love?
- What action is love taking in the song?
- Does the song describe love as a feeling?
- Is love portrayed as a positive experience or as a problem?

You may add other questions based on the songs you select.

Finally, at the last station where 1 Corinthians 13 is heard, ask how this portrayal of love differs from what they have heard in the secular love songs.

This activity can be wrapped up by discussing what the world believes love is and what God says love is. Point out that the world sees love as a feeling that is often temporary and self-centered. Compare this to what God says love is in 1 Corinthians 13. Let them make conclusions about the difference between the different messages about love.

Monument Reminders

SPECIAL FEATURES

NUMBER

PREP TIME

10-20 MINUTES

TIME REQUIRED

30-60 MINUTES

MATERIALS NEEDED

Natural materials

PREPARATION

Gather the materials needed to make the monument. If you choose one of the variations, make sure you have the required materials.

WHAT TO DO

In the Bible there are several incidents of building a monument in honor of an important event, such as when Jacob made a monument to remember his covenant with his father-in-law Laban (see Genesis 31:46), or when God instructed the Israelites to build a monument out of 12 stones after they safely crossed the Jordan River (see Joshua 4:1-7). These places were memorialized to remind them of the special event that took place there.

Why not initiate the same practice with your youth as you make trips or go on retreats? With little disruption to the environment, you can gather some rocks or sticks or other natural items, build an altar and have your closing service. If appropriate, you can dismantle the altar following the service, or let it remain for visits in future years. One youth group did such a thing at the beginning of the summer and many of the students revisited it over that summer for private prayers.

This activity gives your group members reminders that focus on the milestones in their spiritual growth. These monumental memories can become sacred reminders of God's continual involvement in their lives. Occasionally asking your students if there are any new spiritual milestones in their lives will emphasize their need to continue to build and grow in their relationships with Him.

Variations

- You could also make a stepping stone out of concrete by using a form made out of two-by-fours nailed together to make a one- to two-foot square. When it is partially dry, write the date and the

event on it. Memorable items may be pressed into the concrete before it is dry. This can be placed in a garden area, used to make a remembrance walk or a patio area for youth to gather for special prayer or dedication services. If you plan to keep these for a long time, brush on a good concrete sealer.

- Inside events need not be overlooked. It is easy to use clay to make a portable monument, or plaster of paris to make a plaque in a box, then peel away the cardboard when the monument is dry. The students can decorate the monument by collecting items from the area of the retreat or special event and pressing them into the clay or plaster of paris. The remembrance monument can then be taken back with the group and placed in the youth meeting area.

- Encourage students to make individual monuments for milestones in their own lives. A great time to do this is when a student accepts Christ as Savior or when he or she makes a major commitment to serve the Lord or a rededication. This can be done by writing the date and milestone event on a small stone, or in a small plaque made of clay or plaster of paris.

SPECIAL FEATURES

NUMBER

PREP TIME

10 MINUTES

TIME REQUIRED

10 MINUTES

Room-Sized Diary

This is an ongoing group diary that is a visible reminder to the youth group throughout the year. It is added to after each meeting, giving the students a sense of where they were, what they have accomplished and where they have gone together during the year. It builds community by helping them see how much they are a part of each others' lives.

MATERIALS NEEDED

A large roll of white paper, the size used in covering tables or bulletin boards
Sturdy tape
Felt-tip pens

PREPARATION

Unroll the large roll of paper and securely tape a continuous strip around the youth room. Because the paper is heavy and will be up for a long time, make certain that it is well attached to the wall with sturdy tape.

WHAT TO DO

Allow the students plenty of time, either after each meeting or before the next meeting, to write capsulized reports on what happened at the meeting or activity. Ask those doing the writing to use their first names or initials to identify themselves and to date their entry. After each group entry, draw a bold, vertical line to separate the dates. Artistic students could also add drawings to the written accounts. Have them add meaningful Scripture verses.

At the end of the year, and occasionally throughout the year, stop and look at the various entries and talk about the unexpected nature of life.

This ongoing diary is a wonderful means to visually show the group how we are all in this life together, and it also helps them recall common experiences and memories.

Variations

- Add prayer requests that can be identified with big, stick-on dots. Record answers to the prayer requests.
- Various wacky prizes can be awarded—perhaps each quarter—to the funniest, strangest, most touching, etc. entries along the way.
- Add a few photos to the diary.

Round Table Roulette

This group builder will require most of a 90-minute meeting to play it as it should be played. It is an eight-round mingling of twosomes, foursomes, open table discussions and entire group responses. In each of the eight rounds, a different sharing or discussion is required to complete the round. Between the rounds, the leaders, time keepers or emcee may invite some "from the floor" responses.

MATERIALS NEEDED

> Five round tables
> Chairs
> An instruction sheet for each student
> A stopwatch
> A loud bell, gong or a pan with a wooden spoon
> Paper and pencil

PREPARATION

Set up five round tables, numbered 1 through 5 with several chairs arranged around each. Rectangular tables are okay if you don't have round ones. On each table, list in large print on a piece of paper the three topics that will be discussed at that table (see Round 4 explanation below).

Prepare the questions for Rounds 4, 5 and 8 and also the instruction sheets for students. Select someone to be the timekeeper who will also give the signal to stop or change.

HOW TO BEGIN

Begin by asking the group to sit down to hear the instructions. Read the following introduction:

> Tonight we are going to have fun, but having fun depends upon each of you. To make this a success, you need to be willing to share a bit about yourself with others in a safe, non-judgmental way. You'll be asked to move around the room and meet new people and get to know old friends better. What you share is voluntary and not threatening. By the end

of the evening, you'll know more about each other and, hopefully, have made some new friends.

Distribute the Round Table Roulette instruction sheets and tell the students that you will lead them through each round; the sheets are simply for reference. Remind them that they need to move quickly at each new round.

THE ROUNDS

ROUND 1 (TWO MINUTES)

Have them quickly divide into pairs, preferably with someone they do not know at all or at least not very well. Tell them to each share for their first 30 seconds about their favorite childhood pet and their second 30 seconds about a favorite vacation spot. They are supposed to each talk for 30 seconds on each of the topics. Tell them you will need to ring a bell (gong or pan) every 30 seconds and they must stop talking and change talkers and/or topics. Each time you give the signal, shout out the reminder of who should be talking and about which topic. The whole round should last two minutes.

ROUND 2 (FOUR MINUTES)

Each duo teams up with another duo to make a foursome. Each of the four shares for 60 seconds talking about:

- Something neat about their childhood;
- A favorite grade school memory; or
- Something they really like about their favorite teacher.

Ring the bell every 60 seconds and remind them to change talkers. The round should take four minutes.

ROUND 3 (FOUR MINUTES)

Each duo trades partners within the foursome, creating a new duo. The new duos share the following for two minutes:

- What life was like in their hometowns as children;
- How their family lives were as they were growing; and
- Their favorite hobbies/interests when they were younger.

Ring the bell every two minutes, reminding them to change talkers. The entire round should last four minutes.

TABLE TOPICS

The following rounds take place at the five round tables. At your five table stations, write a large number, from one to five, on a sheet of 8½x11-inch paper and put it on the table. Then on three different colored sheets of paper, write the three topics for that table, depending on the round (i.e, Round 4 topics on blue paper, Round 5 topics on yellow paper and Round 8 topics on green paper).

You can allow students to choose the topics of interest to them. If that results in students choosing topics according to what their friends choose, you might want to have them pick numbers or count off by fives. Each table should have an adult discussion leader to facilitate the topic with easy questions and ideas.

If students are allowed to choose a topic of interest to them, you must reserve the right to "redistribute the wealth" of students. Allow the students five minutes or so to talk per round, but ring the bell well before their interest wanes.

ROUND 4 (APPROXIMATELY FIVE MINUTES)

On blue paper (8½x11-inch is fine) write the following topics for Round 4:

> Table 1: What is faith?
> Table 2: What do you think about present world political events?
> Table 3: What is your personal philosophy of life?
> Table 4: What is wrong with the world?
> Table 5: What is right with the world?

These topics may be adapted to your group's needs, interests or the theme of the meeting, but make the topics fairly equal and representative of the interests of the students, or one table may have 90 percent of the group and others may be empty.

ROUND 5 (FIVE TO EIGHT MINUTES)

On each of five yellow sheets of paper, write one of the following topics for Round 5:

> Table 1: Current movies/TV shows
> Table 2: Talk radio hosts: Dr. Laura Schlessinger, Howard Stern and Rush Limbaugh
> Table 3: Sports Teams
> Table 4: Music Videos
> Table 5: TV Talk Shows

Prepare a few leading questions for adult table leaders to spark the discussion. For example: Which is your favorite movie (team, talk show, etc.) and why? Which is the worst movie (team, talk show, etc.) and why? What did you watch on TV last night? Was it worth your time? Who's your favorite person on the team?

Ring the bell after about five to eight minutes. Monitor to insure that the students are still on target. If a group is in a jam, assign the table discussion leader some rescue questions to keep the discussion rolling.

RETURN TO PAIRS AND FOURSOMES

ROUND 6 (FOUR MINUTES)
Have everyone find their original partner from the first duo. Give each partner two minutes to catch up and report on interesting things he or she may have learned or heard in rounds three through five. Ring the bell every two minutes and remind them to change talkers.

ROUND 7 (EIGHT MINUTES)
Return to the original foursome and allow each member to discuss:

> Ideas for a closer walk with Christ
> Ideas for strengthening the youth program
> What they like best about the youth group

Ask one student in each foursome to take notes on ideas, complaints, concerns and joys. Be sure to collect their notes. Ring the bell every two minutes and remind them to change talkers.

RETURN TO TABLE TOPICS

ROUND 8 (APPROXIMATELY FIVE MINUTES)
On each of five green sheets of paper write one of the following topics for Round 8:

> Table 1: The best thing about being a teenager
> Table 2: The greatest problem troubling our society
> Table 3: What you are learning about Jesus
> Table 4: What God has been teaching you recently
> Table 5: How you are successfully dealing with your parents

Ring the bell after five or so minutes. Before closing the meeting, gather the group in a prayer circle and thank God for the varieties of

human beings, human experiences and the ability to share our lives with others along this faith walk.

Incidentally, this activity works famously during winter break meetings of college-age students who have not seen each other for some time. It also serves as a good kickoff for a retreat.

Round Table Roulette Instruction Sheet

Each time you here the bell ring, stop talking and listen for directions.

ROUND 1 (TWO MINUTES)
Form pairs and discuss each of the following topics for 30 seconds:

- A favorite childhood pet
- A favorite vacation spot

When you hear the signal, stop talking and listen for instructions.

ROUND 2 (FOUR MINUTES)
Team up with another pair to make a foursome. Each of you shares for 60 seconds on one of the following topics:

- Something neat about your childhood;
- A favorite grade school memory; or
- Something you really like about your favorite teacher.

When you hear the signal, stop talking and listen for instructions.

ROUND 3 (FOUR MINUTES)
Trade partners within your foursome, creating new pairs. Each partner shares on the following for two minutes each:

- What life was like in your hometown as a child;
- How your family life was while growing; and
- Your favorite hobbies/interests when you were younger.

When you hear the signal, stop talking and listen for instructions.

ROUND 4 (APPROXIMATELY FIVE MINUTES)
Choose one of the table topics listed on the blue sheets at each table. Join the group at that table to discuss your topic:

Table 1: What is faith?
Table 2: What do you think about present world political events?

Table 3: What is your personal philosophy of life?
Table 4: What is wrong with the world?
Table 5: What is right with the world?

When you hear the signal, stop talking and listen for instructions.

ROUND 5 (FIVE TO EIGHT MINUTES)

Choose one of the table topics listed on the yellow sheet. Join the group at that table to discuss the topic.

Table 1: Current movies/TV shows
Table 2: Talk radio hosts: Dr. Laura Schlessinger,
 Howard Stern and Rush Limbaugh
Table 3: Sports Teams
Table 4: Music Videos
Table 5: TV Talk Shows

When you hear the signal, stop talking and listen for instructions.

ROUND 6 (TWO MINUTES)

Find your first partner, pair up and discuss interesting things you've learned or heard in any of your discussions.
 When you hear the signal, stop talking and listen for instructions.

ROUND 7 (EIGHT MINUTES)

Return to your original foursome and discuss the following:

Ideas for a closer walk with Christ
Ideas for strengthening the youth program
What they like best about the youth group

Have one person in your foursome write down ideas. When you hear the signal, stop talking and listen for instructions.

ROUND 8 (APPROXIMATELY FIVE MINUTES)

Choose one of the table topics listed on the green sheet. Join the group at that table to discuss the topic.

Table 1: The best thing about being a teenager
Table 2: The greatest problem troubling our society
Table 3: What you are learning about Jesus
Table 4: What God has been teaching you recently
Table 5: How you are successfully dealing with your parents

When you hear the signal, stop talking and listen for instructions.

Secret ID

Teenagers are often fascinated by the accounts of the Early Church gathering for worship during persecution under threat of death or arrest. They seem to love the idea that early believers used the sign of the fish drawn in the sand as a means of identification with the Body of Christ before entering a worship service.

WHAT TO DO

Let your students invent a similar identification symbol for access to youth group meetings. The symbol may change from group to group, year-to-year, but the point is that students can say, "I am part of this group because I know the secret entry symbol." Guests and visitors are exempted from this ritual, but what a way to let them know they are part of the group when they return and are admitted using the sign.

The sign should be created by the students themselves—a secret handshake, walking into the meeting room backwards, a symbol or letter drawn with a fingertip in the back of the entry guard, one sleeve rolled up, etc.—just as long as it is their idea.

Historically, such gestures held great meaning and confirmed that the person was indeed a part of the group. Students need to be assured of membership and their identity in any group. This is one small way of giving that security.

Seven Stations Mixer

This building activity gathers players into shared responses to seven questions. Then, in the group, they share a few more details of why they answered as they did.

MATERIALS NEEDED

Seven $8^1/_2$ x 11-inch pieces of paper
Felt-tip pens
Photocopies of the questions you develop

PREPARATION

Prepare the room for this activity by taping the numerals 1 through 7 on the walls around the room on $8^1/_2$ x 11-inch pieces of paper. These numbers indicate the seven stations that will correspond with the answers of each question. Prepare a sheet with a set of seven questions with seven answers for each question. These questions can be lead-ins for your meeting theme. Make photocopies of the question sheets, one for each student attending.

WHAT TO DO

As the students gather, give everyone a sheet of questions and a pen or pencil. Explain that they are to answer the questions quietly at their seats without talking to anyone else. Don't tell them about the numbers on the wall or some will answer the questions identically so that they can stand together with their friends when the answers are being shared. Give them a few minutes to answer each of the seven questions.

After they have completed the questions, ask all of the students who answered the first question with answer 1 to stand under the number 1, so on through answer 7. Once at the stations, instruct each one of them to share why they answered as they did.

Sample Question

Circle the person who most supported you as you were growing up.

1. Your mom
2. Your dad
3. Your grandma
4. Your grandpa
5. A sibling
6. A neighbor
7. A friend

After the students gather at the number corresponding to their answers, they will discuss why this person was such a great support. For example, all of the students who gather under number 4 will tell why grandpa was such a great support.

Follow this same procedure with the rest of the questions and answers.

Questions can be about anything: hobbies, politics, Bible characters, sports, pets, etc. They can be serious or trivial. What is important is that the questions bring the group to a new level of sharing and understanding, giving them new topics of common interest with one another.

Small Group Questions

Choose a Scripture verse, a news item, a quote or any single topic question. Place the students in small groups with four to six members to discuss it. This could be done in place of a warm-up activity or a meeting opening by immediately assigning students to small groups as they walk into the room. It is a good alternative to letting them gather and chat and staying only in groups of friends. Let the groups discuss for no more than 10 minutes or the novelty will wear off.

Special Interest Groups

SPECIAL
FEATURES

NUMBER

PREP TIME

VARIABLE

TIME REQUIRED

60+ MINUTES

DEVELOPING A MINISTRY USING YOUR PERSONAL GIFTS OR INTERESTS

Some years ago a youth pastor responded to the many wishes of his youth groups to give group guitar lessons. Originally, it began as a way for him to meet the insistent wishes of the students in one fell swoop. However, it became something more—it enhanced the youth group and provided a service for the church.

Guitar Choir now meets every Monday for one hour after school throughout the school year. The youth pastor teaches the students basic guitar skills with the understanding that his time is valuable and since the lessons are free, there needs to be a fair payback. The payback resulted in something the students really enjoy—playing guitar as a group for various church events.

The Guitar Choir plays for the regular worship services, Youth Sunday and the annual church business meeting. They accompany the youth pastor on visits to the early childhood Sunday School classes and Children's Chapel. The Guitar Choir plays when the youth visit soup kitchens or other churches. They also lead the singing time at youth group meetings. Of course, the selection of songs is equal to the skills of the students involved, but the congregation and the students don't know the difference.

The ministry of the Guitar Choir has seen miraculous results. Junior and senior high students begin to step out as leaders as they gain confidence in learning a skill and performing for others. The Guitar Choir has become a great example of how ministry can succeed by using the various spiritual gifts of the group members. It also gives students a feeling of belonging to the whole church body when they can be integrated into its ministries in some way.

Guitar Choir has also been a wonderful tool for community evangelism among the unchurched youth. Students bring their guitar-playing friends to join the group. Not surprisingly, students who have trouble asking a friend to church have no difficulty asking a friend to come play guitar.

Special interest groups within the youth group, such as a Guitar

Choir, have strong unity-building effects. The small group setting has long been recognized for building community as it builds a bridge into the whole group. The challenge of learning a task together is also a bonding agent. Serving others through what is being learned is a great way to incorporate a sense of ministry. And students who don't shine in any other areas often find a home in the youth group through the Guitar Choir.

You can adapt this Guitar Choir philosophy to any area of skill or ability you or other youth workers have. One youth worker uses the same idea with a leaded glass crafts group he leads. It takes little imagination to come up with other applications.

Suggestions for Variations

Vocal Choir   Service/Missions Group
Drama Club   Computer Club
Puppeteers   Community Service Group
Combined Performance Groups   Sports Teams
Cooking School   Aerobics Class
Hiking Club   Any Craft or Hobby
Nature/Environmental Group   Individual Sports (i.e., tennis, golf, etc.)

Your Eulogy

SPECIAL FEATURES

NUMBER

PREP TIME

NONE

TIME REQUIRED

15-20 MINUTES

This activity takes about two minutes to introduce, five minutes for each participant to complete and about 10 minutes (depending on group size) to complete.

MATERIALS NEEDED

Paper
Pens or pencils

WHAT TO DO

Begin by asking: "How do you want to be remembered? Strangely enough, folks who have achieved great deeds in life often reflect that their accomplishments don't fully express who they really are inside—only what they have done.

"A eulogy is a message shared at a funeral that serves to remind the gathered mourners about the life of the person who has died. Eulogies summarize the person's life by sharing what he or she is likely to be remembered for.

"What should be said about your life thus far? What do you believe and stand for? What is important to you? This is your chance to tell us who you really are by writing your own eulogy. Be honest and open and don't hold back. This isn't boasting—it's honestly evaluating how you see yourself and who you are on the inside."

Distribute pens or pencils, and paper. Give the students a few minutes to write a short eulogy. Allow time for each person to share his or her eulogy.

Variation

Have students write inscriptions for their tombstones. Ask: "If you lived your life the way you would like to, how would you like to be remembered by those whose lives you touch? What would you like to have inscribed on your tombstone?"

Give students a few minutes to write their inscriptions, then have a time of group sharing.

Indexes

Topical Guide

GAMES

Group Games

Impromptu Games

CROWDBREAKERS

COMMUNITY BUILDERS

Preparation Times

GAMES

Minutes	Name of the Game	Page

CROWDBREAKERS

COMMUNITY BUILDERS

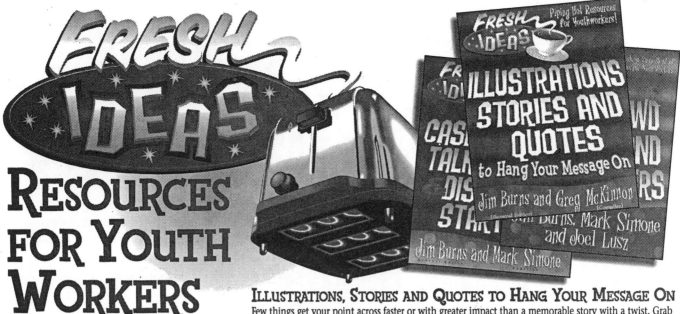

RESOURCES FOR YOUTH WORKERS

Jim Burns, General Editor

Turn your youth group meetings into dynamic, exciting events that kids look forward to attending week after week! Supercharge your messages, grab their attention with your activities and connect with kids the first time and every time with these great resources. Just try to keep these books on the shelf!

ILLUSTRATIONS, STORIES AND QUOTES TO HANG YOUR MESSAGE ON

Few things get your point across faster or with greater impact than a memorable story with a twist. Grab your teens' attention by talking with your mouth full of unforgettable stories.
Manual, ISBN 08307.18834 $16.99

CASE STUDIES, TALK SHEETS AND DISCUSSION STARTERS

Teens learn best when they talk—not when you talk at them. A discussion allowing youth to discover the truth for themselves, with your guidance, is a powerful experience that will stay with them for a lifetime.
Manual, ISBN 08307.18842 $16.99

GAMES, CROWDBREAKERS AND COMMUNITY BUILDERS

Dozens of innovative, youth-group-tested ideas for fun and original crowdbreakers, as well as successful plans and trips for building a sense of community in your group.
Manual, ISBN 08307.18818 $16.99

More Resources for Youth Workers, Parents & Students

NATIONAL INSTITUTE OF YOUTH MINISTRY — NIYM

Steering Them Straight
Stephen Arterburn & Jim Burns

Parents can find understanding as well as practical tools to deal with crisis situations. Includes guidelines that will help any family prevent problems before they develop.
UPC 156179.4066 $10.99

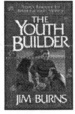

The Youth Builder
Jim Burns

This Gold Medallion Award winner provides you with proven methods, specific recommendations and hands-on examples of handling and understanding the problems and challenges of youth ministry.
ISBN 089081.1576. $16.95

Spirit Wings
Jim Burns

In the language of today's teens, these 84 short devotionals will encourage youth to build a stronger and more intimate relationship with God.
ISBN 08928.37837 $10.95

Radical Love
Book & Video, Jim Burns

In *Radical Love* kids discover why it's best to wait on God's timing, how to say no when their bodies say yes and how to find forgiveness for past mistakes.
Paperback, ISBN 08307.17935 $9.99
VHS Video, SPCN 85116.00922 $19.99

90 Days Through the New Testament
Jim Burns

A growth experience through the New Testament that lays the foundation for developing a daily time with God.
ISBN 08307.14561 $9.99

Getting in Touch with God
Jim Burns

Develop a consistent and disciplined tim with God in the midst of hectic schedules as Jim Burns shares with you inspiring devotional readings to deepen you love of God.
ISBN 08908.15208 $2.95

Radical Christianity
Book & Video, Jim Burns

Radical Christianity is a proven plan to help youth live a life that's worth living and make a difference in their world.
Paperback, ISBN 08307.17927 $9.99
VHS Video, SPCN 85116.01082 $19.99

The Youth Worker's Book of Case Studies
Jim Burns

Fifty-two true stories with discussion questions to add interest to Bible studies.
ISBN 08307.15827 $12.99

Add a New Member to Your Youth Staff.

Jim Burns is President of the National Institute of Youth Ministry.

Meet Jim Burns. He won't play guitar and he doesn't do windows, but he will take care of your programming needs. That's because his new curriculum, **YouthBuilders Group Bible Studies,** is a comprehensive program designed to take your group through their high school years. (If you have junior high kids in your group, **YouthBuilders** works for them too.)

For less than $6 a month, you'll get Jim Burns' special recipe of high-involvement, discussion-oriented, Bible-centered studies. It's the next generation of Bible curriculum for youth—and with Jim on your staff, you'll be free to spend more time one-on-one with the kids in your group.

Here are some of Youth-Builders' hottest features:

- Reproducible pages—one book fits your whole group
- Wide appeal—big groups, small groups—even adjusts to combine junior high/high school groups
- Hits home—special section to involve parents with every session of the study
- Interactive Bible discovery—geared to help young people find answers themselves
- Cheat sheets—a Bible *Tuck-In*™ with all the session information on a single page
- Flexible format—perfect for Sunday mornings, midweek youth meetings, or camps and retreats
- Three studies in one—each study has three four-session modules that examine critical life choices.

   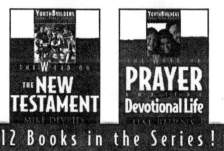  

12 Books in the Series!

The Word on Sex, Drugs & Rock 'N' Roll
ISBN 08307.16424 $16.99

The Word on Prayer and the Devotional Life
ISBN 08307.16432 $16.99

The Word on the Basics of Christianity
ISBN 08307.16440 $16.99

The Word on Being a Leader, Serving Others & Sharing Your Faith
ISBN 08307.16459 $16.99

The Word on Helping Friends in Crisis
ISBN 08307.16467 $16.99

The Word on the Life of Jesus
ISBN 08307.16475 $16.99

The Word on Finding and Using Your Spiritual Gifts
ISBN 08307.17897 $16.99

The Word on the Sermon on the Mount
ISBN 08307.17234 $16.99

The Word on Spiritual Warfare
ISBN 08307.17242 $16.99

The Word on the New Testament
ISBN 08307.17250 $16.99

The Word on the Old Testament
ISBN 08307.17269 $16.99

The Word on Family
ISBN 08307.17277 $16.99

More Great Resources from Jim Burns

Drugproof Your Kids
Stephen Arterburn and Jim Burns
Solid biblical principles are combined with the most effective prevention and intervention techniques to give parents a guide they can trust.
ISBN 08307.17714 $10.99

Drugproof Your Kids Video
A 90-minute seminar featuring Stephen Arterburn and Jim Burns. Includes a reproducible syllabus.
SPCN 85116.00876 $19.99

Parenting Teens Positively Video *Featuring Jim Burns*
Understand the forces shaping the world of a teenager and what you can do to be a positive influence. This powerful message of hope is for anyone working with—or living with—youth. Includes reproducible syllabus. UPC 607135.000655 $29.99

Surviving Adolescence
Jim Burns
Jim Burns helps teens—and their parents—negotiate the path from adolescence to adulthood with real-life stories that show how to make it through the teen years in one piece. ISBN 08307.20650 $9.99

For these and more great resources and to learn about NIYM's leadership training, call **1-800-397-9725.**

Gospel Light

What in the world is *NIYM*?

A.) The Neurotically Inclined Yo-Yo Masters

B.) The Neatest Incidental Yearbook Mystery

C.) The Natural Ignition Yields of Marshmallows

D.) The National Institute of Youth Ministry

If you deliberately picked *A*, *B*, or *C* you're the reason Jim Burns started NIYM! If you picked *D*, you can go to the next page. In any case, you could learn more about NIYM. Here are some IQ score-raisers:

Jim Burns started NIYM to:
• Meet the growing needs of training and equipping youth workers and parents
• Develop excellent resources and events for young people—in the U.S. and internationally
• Empower young people and their families to make wise decisions and experience a vital Christian lifestyle.

NIYM can make a difference in your life and enhance your youth work skills through these special events:

Institutes—These consist of week-long, in-depth small-group training sessions for youth workers.

Trainer of Trainees—NIYM will train you to train others. You can use this training with your volunteers, parents and denominational events. You can go through the certification process and become an official NIYM associate. (No, you don't get a badge or decoder ring).

International Training—Join NIYM associates to bring youth ministry to kids and adults around the world. (You'll learn meanings to universal words like "yo!" and "hey!")

Custom Training—These are special training events for denominational groups, churches, networks, colleges and seminaries.

Parent Forums—We'll come to your church or community with two incredible hours of learning, interaction and fellowship. It'll be fun finding out who makes your kids tick!

Youth Events—Dynamic speakers, interaction and drama bring a powerful message to kids through a fun and fast-paced day. Our youth events include: This Side Up, Radical Respect, Surviving Adolescence and Peer Leadership.

For brain food or a free information packet about the National Institute of Youth Ministry, write to:

NIYM

P.O. Box 4374 • San Clemente, CA 92674

Tel: (714) 498-4418 • Fax: (714) 498-0037 • NIYMin@aol.com